TEAMS
That Work

The Six Characteristics
of High Performing Teams

Tom Champoux · Cliff Chirls · George Myers

CONTENTS

PREFACE

After spending decades working with both effective and ineffective teams, we couldn't help but see patterns, both for what made teams successful and what derailed them. This book illustrates what we observed in patterns of successful teams, namely how certain key attributes or characteristics are present and working together.

We wrote this book to give you a rich awareness of the characteristics of high-performing teams in a way that is useable and actionable. This is not a handbook or a manual, but rather a guide toward a deeper approach to concepts that inform leaders how to create effective teams. If you're currently leading or on a high-performance team, you will undoubtedly recognize the strong presence of these characteristics. If you're leading or on a team that could use some help, you will find information that can help you identify specific ways to improve team performance.

Before we started writing *Teams That Work* we interviewed numerous leaders from eight organizations, including The Boeing Company, Bank of Hawaii, Cornell University School of Hotel Administration, Loews Corporation, the NCAA, Fiat Chrysler Automobiles, H.R. Spinner Corporation and the Facility for Rare Isotope Beams at Michigan State University. Our purpose was to hear their stories and learn how the six characteristics in the Teams That Work model were reflected in their respective cultures. The book includes examples based on what we heard in the interviews, as well as stories about work we've done over the years with other companies and organizations (some of which will go unnamed by their preference).

Although we isolated the six characteristics in our own research, the stories we heard made it clear how interconnected these characteristics truly are. At every company and organization, every person we spoke with revealed ways in which all the characteristics are woven throughout the fabric of the work they do, so even though we feature one organization at the beginning of each characteristic all the organizations represent and demonstrate all six characteristics. Whether you're building jets or automobiles, conducting high-tech research, providing financial services, education or hospitality, or overseeing collegiate athletics the work is accomplished by people working together. We hope you will be inspired, just as we were, to bring these characteristics to life in your team and organization.

Special thanks for the generous time of the organizations and individuals we spoke with. In addition, we would like to express our deep appreciation for all the individuals in the organizations we have been fortunate to work with over the years as well as the team members who have worked at the Effectiveness Institute. This book would not have been possible without you. Finally, thanks to Sue Mills for the generous use of her "Creamsicle Cottage" for a writing retreat and Mary Myers for editing assistance.

FOREWORD

High School, History and Gratitude

Founders Dr. Bill Maynard's and Tom Champoux's adventure started not long after they met while working together at Cleveland High School in downtown Seattle. Both were high energy, positive risk-takers who loved kids. Bill was serving as the youngest principal in school district history, and Tom taught language arts, a class with a mile-long waiting list. From the perspective of a career path, things looked pretty rosy… until you went a little deeper.

At that time Cleveland had a lot of highs, and we don't mean the good kind. It had the highest dropout rate, the highest absentee rate, the highest suspension rate, and the highest number of incidents involving violence and vandalism. Of Seattle's 12 high schools, Cleveland was perceived as the "loser." This was compounded every morning by two facts: kids pouring off school buses and entering a decaying old brick building and the reality that these same kids played on Cleveland's sports teams, which were perpetually trounced by every other school in the conference.

'Rosy' expectations were a perennial illusion; this was a challenge of all challenges – a loser image, a decaying building, a tired faculty that had minimal district support and little hope for a more positive future. It was nothing short of an educator's worst nightmare. When the district's superintendent hired Bill as Principal, he gave him one single directive: "Don't have a riot!" He wasn't kidding.

Bill, Tom, and a handful of others found a connection in wanting to change things, wanting Cleveland to be something different – a safe place where relationships were formed, pride was developed and skills were learned. They quickly realized that business-as-usual wasn't working at Cleveland. Control, force and fear – the usual tools used for transformation – could not change student behavior and performance, at least not for the better. A different approach was needed, so they started with the end in mind. The culture change they sought began with an obvious statement:

"If what you're doing isn't working, change what you're doing."

And… the only way to do things differently was to be courageous.

Now, no old guard likes the new infusion of energy that comes with youth and desire. That means change, and, predictably, most of the staff resisted, clinging to "the way we've always done it." But Bill and Tom found the curious few who could and would help make a difference… and the change began.

Adding to this new courageous approach, Bill and Tom did the unthinkable. They enlisted the help of the students. They began involving students in problem-solving and decision-making teams with those brave staff members who were willing to participate. Bill and Tom figured a few "supporters" were better than none, and it was their challenge to inspire those few into champions of the cause. (It was the '70s of course and 'causes' were quite common.)

On the weekends, offsite retreats at Mount Rainier were scheduled for students who wanted to be part of something better. Communication skills and conflict resolution were the focus areas. Listening skills were taught and practiced. Problem-solving models were shared and role-played. The values of trust, respect, dignity and integrity were surfaced, discussed and agreed to as a pathway for change, for creating a new and better way of doing things.

With these skills in hand, collaboration and teamwork became the primary vehicles for change. Being "right" or having the most power were no longer the singular driving forces. As the culture evolved and the level of trust and respect increased, so did the level of pride students took in themselves and in their school. Instead of graffiti-covered walls, the halls were decorated with student-created artwork and proud illustrations of the Cleveland Eagle, the school mascot. Life-skills courses were added to the high school curriculum. Values were stressed and measurement improvements were made to the way performance was evaluated for both students and teachers. Results became visible, and as they did, more and more teachers participated. The culture of Cleveland High School began to shift.

During the next few years, the Cleveland pendulum swung. The school went from the highest absentee rate in the city to the lowest. It dropped from the highest rate of suspensions and drop-outs to the lowest. The football team had its first non-losing season. (Sportswriters elected the coach, Jim Sampson, "Coach of the Year" for winning four games.) The next season, Cleveland went on to the playoffs. And the basketball team placed third in the state tournament before winning back-to-back state championships.

The high school's overall transformation received so much attention and generated so much visibility that national television stations covered it and Principal Bill Maynard, was selected as the "Newsmaker of Tomorrow" by *Time* magazine.

FROM SCHOOL TO BUSINESS

That courage, coupled with the philosophies and strategies that Bill and Tom used to transform Cleveland High School were not a fluke. In fact, it was their insight that caused the two to wonder, "If we can create grand transformation in a high school, why can't we do it in business?"

And so they formed the Effectiveness Institute to bring the first-hand knowledge that came from their experience to the corporate world. In a few years the Effectiveness Institute had acquired clients around the globe, and the thinking behind Bill and Tom's original work at Cleveland High School was used as part of a growing collection of intellectual property. These programs and tools were developed and continue to be updated and augmented to facilitate positive and quantifiable change for many national and international companies.

CHAPTER ONE

Teams That Work

Just three short simple words, but we know how difficult creating an effective team can be. Still, results that fit this description do happen. You've seen it – an amateur or professional sports team that wins despite the odds makers' judgments. Or the team of scientists that makes a major breakthrough despite the experts' contrary statements. Or the group of soldiers that survives despite theoretically overwhelming numbers. Something indescribable, but nevertheless indisputable, can occur through teamwork. A favorite business example of ours comes from the "desktop publishing revolution".

Few people know or remember, but Apple's Macintosh initially was a dud. Its sales were poor at best and many people doubted it would ever succeed because it relied on a graphical user interface that critics condemned as "toy-like" and "wasteful of computational resources".

In fact, the poor sales performance caused then CEO John Sculley to fire Founder Steve Jobs in September 1985. That same year, the three "A's" as they were called – Apple, Adobe and Aldus – teamed up to dramatically change Apple's fortunes.

Apple developed the LaserWriter, a desktop printer. Adobe developed the Postscript language, which allowed the LaserWriter to print a variety of fonts, and Aldus developed publishing software PageMaker, which ran on the Macintosh.

Collaboration by these three companies and their products which were designed to work together, allowed individuals, businesses and other organizations to self-publish a wide range of printed matter – from menus and newsletters to books, magazines and newspapers – without the prohibitive expense of commercial printing. Until that point, typesetting equipment, costing hundreds of thousands of dollars, was required to do any serious publishing. This multi-company approach solved a significant problem for a fraction of that cost.

Needless to say, sales of the Macintosh computer soared. Adobe became a major player in printing and viewing documents. Aldus' software product, PageMaker, became the standard for "desktop publishing" (a phrase coined by the CEO of Aldus, Paul Brainerd), and this revolution in technology brought publishing of information to the masses. Teamwork between the three "A's" paid off for everyone.

THE TEAMS THAT WORK MODEL

Nearly everyone has experienced what it's like to be on both effective and ineffective teams. While being on an effective team is more satisfying and rewarding for team members, it also produces better results.

Through our 35 years of work and research we've identified the six characteristics of effective teams, which we call the Teams That Work model. Revealing these characteristics makes them available for teams to consider and discuss, focusing the conversation on ways to improve performance. The six characteristics include:

1. High level of trust.
2. High level of respect.
3. Commitment to a clear and common purpose.

4.   Willingness and ability to manage conflict.

5.   Focus on results.

6.   Alignment of authority and accountability.

One important note: this is a living model, which means we are constantly looking for ways to enhance it by integrating the latest research and observations. For example, the last iteration of the model occurred in 2012 when we altered some of the questions in our Teams That Work assessment to be consistent with the validation studies we contracted with external academic experts to conduct.

FINDING BALANCE

One of the challenges teams face in improving their performance is targeting the discussion. This is where the greatest value of the model is found. When used as a framework for dialogue, it helps create more objective and constructive conversations to improve team performance.

To provide context, at the highest descriptive level of every team there are two basic elements: Tasks and People. We look at these elements using the "yin-yang" model, which can be thought of as complementary forces interacting to form a dynamic system in which the whole is greater than the parts.

Every team has tasks they need to do and people (i.e., team members) who interact to accomplish those tasks. What are the risks when a team member is brilliant at task accomplishment but can't collaborate effectively with others? Likewise, what is the value to the team when a member can get along with everyone but underperforms?

These mismatches demonstrate the kinds of imbalances that impact performance, cause animosity, missed deadlines, and increased frustration in the workplace.

Before we dig into the details on these characteristics there are two other important variables we need to mention that have a big impact on team performance: behavior patterns and the behavior of the leader. We'll explain what we mean by behavior patterns next and address the aspect of the leader in Chapter 8.

BEHAVIOR PATTERNS

The focus here is on the different, but nevertheless predictable ways people tend to behave. We call these tendencies *behavior patterns*. Although this book focuses on six characteristics of Teams That Work, we need to recognize behavior patterns have a significant impact on those characteristics.

Let's start by thinking about your own behavior…

- Do you tend to talk quickly or carefully?

- Is your body language demonstrative or reserved?

- Are your comments at work focused more on the task itself or on how the people doing the task are feeling about it?

- Do you tend to prefer getting something "close enough" and then correcting as you go, or waiting until it's perfect before it gets released?

- Do you tend to make direct or indirect eye contact when talking with someone?

- When you write emails, do you easily use emoticons and exclamation points, or tend to avoid using them?

The answers to these types of questions create an observable pattern of behavior. We've created a four-quadrant model that illustrates how the patterns appear:

- Directing, which primarily focuses on results.

- Influencing, which primarily focuses on people.

- Supporting, which primarily focuses on relationships.

- Analyzing, which primarily focuses on quality, accuracy and perfection.

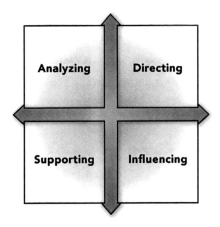

People demonstrate all the behavior patterns but tend to prefer one or two, and it's these varying preferences that impact team performance. Each behavior pattern provides something essential for team success, but the differences can also create unproductive conflict.

Behavior patterns are important and we can't do justice to the richness of this topic in such a brief space (the subject needs its own book!). But we mention it because it is a significant variable and as you read on you'll see these patterns referenced again and again.

Note: At the end of each chapter we've provided a brief summary of the key points followed by questions to help you and your team delve further into each characteristic.

KEY POINTS – TEAMS THAT WORK

Teams That Work is based on a model of six characteristics of high-performing teams. The degrees to which the six characteristics are present indicate how well the team performs. At a macro level, strong team performance requires balancing both Task, or technical skills, and People, or relational skills. The Teams That Work model helps teams determine how to find and maintain an effective balance between the Task and People aspects of performance.

Among the variables that impact team performance, there are two critical ones addressed in this book: behavior patterns and the behavior of the leader. These two variables will be seen throughout the discussion of the six key characteristics:

1. High level of trust.

2. High level of respect.

3. Commitment to a clear and common purpose.

4. Willingness and ability to manage conflict.

5. Focus on results.

6. Alignment of authority and accountability.

QUESTIONS ABOUT TEAMS THAT WORK

Before learning more about the six characteristics, which one do you think your team is currently doing well? Why do you have that perception?

On which of the six characteristics do you think your team needs the most work? What experiences have created that perception?

How is your current team doing at balancing both Task and People skills? Does it focus on one more than the other? If so, what is the impact?

Based on the brief descriptions of the different behavior patterns, which quadrant, or quadrants, do you believe you prefer? Which quadrants do you think your fellow team members prefer? What are the implications for team performance?

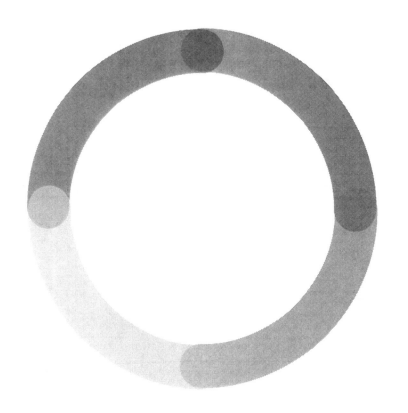

CHAPTER TWO

High Level of Trust

Trust is elusive. You're either trusting, earning trust or losing trust. It can be earned, it can be cultivated and it can be lost. Some trust easily, others not so much. However you look at giving or getting trust, the fact that "trust" appears in one form or another on virtually every organization's list of values is one of the clearest indications of its importance. After all, who does business with someone they don't trust? And who can work openly with a team member they can't trust? Organizations and individuals recognize its importance, but how do you build and sustain something as subjective and dynamic as trust? Adding to the complexity, trust is an outcome, something we develop and build based on factors revealed in the stories that follow.

AN ISLAND SURPRISE

Among the many measures of success for a financial services company is the "Forbes Top Performing Banks" by *Forbes Magazine*. As you can imagine, ranking high in the top 100 is a coveted spot matched with a sweet set of bragging rights for those firms fortunate enough to reach those heights.

The competition is fierce and the metrics of asset quality, capital adequacy and profitability of the 100 largest publicly traded banks and thrifts are reviewed and judged with cold precision. If a bank does achieve this distinction, it would be unusual for it to reap the reward of a high ranking twice in a row. Three times would be remarkable, and four… well now you're just being ridiculous. Oh, and did we mention this was 2009-2012, which has come to be known as the worst financial crisis in U.S. history?

In the heat of the meltdown, one bank maintained its first or second place ranking out of the 100 top performing financial institutions for four years. This was not a money center bank in New York, Chicago or Los Angeles. It was not a large regional bank in Texas or another area of the country which wasn't as negatively impacted by the recession. This was an island bank in the city of Honolulu.

The Bank of Hawaii opened for business with $400,000 in capital in 1897. Its first office was a two-story wooden building in downtown Honolulu. Today, Bank of Hawaii is the largest independent financial services institution in Hawaii, with assets in excess of $13 billion.

Are you thinking "Yes, but that's Hawaii. Where else are you going to bank?" We thought that too. But it turns out customers have plenty of choices – 87 banks, to be exact, are listed as doing business in Hawaii. Yet, Bank of Hawaii garners 50 percent of banking customers in the Hawaiian Islands.

Why? Well, that's what we wanted to know.

CHANGING THE CULTURE

Performance of this caliber clearly is rooted in its culture and leadership. But, mind you, this is a bank, not a dynamic, fast-pivoting technology company positioning itself for an IPO.

No, Bank of Hawaii has a rich history in "top-down" management, meaning the senior managers made all the operational and credit decisions, gave direction to subordinates to a level of detail that gave little if any choices on implementation, and then awaited the results. While this approach is not uncommon, it never pans out as a great solution for garnering trust and respect from employees.

Peter Ho, the current CEO of the bank, told us why he believed that the business required a different approach, "We had to cross our lending and wealth management organizations in order to grow beyond our 50 percent market share in Hawaii. We couldn't do that with a 'command and control' structure. We needed to distribute responsibility and trust people's judgment at all levels of the bank."

According to Carrie Jeanne Oda, the Executive Vice President of Customer and Business Processes and a 24-year veteran of the bank, the bank's legacy has been markedly different. The old style leadership has been replaced by much more collaboration, respect for the opinions of all employees and a requirement for participation in the decision-making process at every level.

Bank of Hawaii made a decision to increase the level of "trusting" it demonstrated toward its employees as part of creating a culture of trust. For example, since the '70s, the credit authority of vice presidents has increased by 1,000 percent. "The change in the culture is considerable," said Alton Kuioka, a seasoned senior executive and most tenured leader at Bank of Hawaii. "It's a management partnership now and not military-like. Employees feel more a part of the organization because management treats people differently."

We spoke to someone from outside the Bank of Hawaii who shed light on what could cause such a significant impact. Ted Teng, President and CEO of The Leading Hotels of the World, Ltd., talked about one aspect of treating people differently when he shared this story. "In my career, the moment of truth was when I learned that a lot of people work at being trustworthy, but the real difficulty is being trusting, which means being the first to exhibit trust. When 'trusting' isn't there, it's not possible to have real trust." If team members are going to build high levels of trust they need to be both trustworthy and trusting.

TRUST ME?

On a practical level, a high level of trust on a team means that all team members are willing to be open with each other. This doesn't mean team members are expected to share personal information or hang out together, but it does mean they share their knowledge, talents, energy and experience with one another to create team success. This is where trusting shows up... and understandably, it is not easy.

What's required is a willingness to be open to sharing one's thinking. That's how you gain access to the wisdom of others attained through experience – both successful and unsuccessful. In practical terms, that means individuals want and need critical thinking applied to their thoughts. And yet, when a tough question is asked as the result of critical thinking, how many times has that question been answered with a new question: "Don't you trust me?" A response like this is a quick way to shut down helpful qualities like transparency and vulnerability. (We'll talk about responses in Chapter 5.)

Openness is about both sharing your thoughts, ideas and experience as well as trusting others when they share their thoughts, ideas and experience. The sustained growth and performance at the Bank of Hawaii resulted from its leaders opening up and changing their ways of demonstrating trust to employees.

So what's required to create trust in a team?

First, there has to be a perception that team members have integrity. That means each team member conducts his or herself with a strong sense of fairness and moral principles that guide their actions. In other words, they do what they say they are going to do and consistently seek to do the right thing. They are focused on helping the team achieve what needs to be accomplished and not on making themselves look good.

Second, team members perceive each other as authentic, meaning they see each other as genuine or real. The opposite of this is considered "two-faced" or fake, which implies false pretense. It's important to recognize that being authentic doesn't mean always acting the same way. People change their behavior based on the variables involved and the situations they are in (think of how everyone demonstrates all the behavior patterns although they tend to prefer one or two).

Third, team members perceive they are cared for. Caring means there is a genuine concern for each other's welfare. This does not mean team members need to be involved in each other's lives outside the workplace, nor does it imply they must share personal information. It does mean they recognize, respect and care about the things that matter to and happen to each other whether it's inside or outside the workplace. Equally, it means they care about the team's performance.

A team we recently worked with had a negative reaction to the idea of caring. Some thought the word "caring" sounded too touchy-feely, too personal. Others said it sounded disingenuous. As the discussion deepened, it became very clear that caring is understood and expressed differently by different people. Which of the following actions most demonstrates caring to you?

1. Attend events together outside of work.

2. Provide a high quality report or document with no errors.

3. Send a team member a personal note with a gift card.

Here are three comparative responses we heard to these three different actions, illustrating how subjective caring can be:

1. "Attending an event outside work together crosses the work/personal life boundary," vs. "I knew my coworkers truly cared about me when they showed up at my concert."

2. "When my coworkers provide me high quality documents for my reports that's a genuine demonstration of caring," vs. "Providing high quality work is part of professional behavior and nothing more than an expected part of the job."

3. "One thing I love about working here is how supportive and caring my boss is. Nearly every month I get a handwritten note from her, sometimes with a little gift card in it," vs. "When people send me gift cards, it's relatively meaningless. Anyone can do that. I feel that people who do that are usually trying to buy my trust."

As you can see, "caring" can look very different from one person to the next. These differences in perceptions are important if you want to be thought of as a person who is genuine and operates with integrity. And yet, if a person does not feel cared about, why would they want to be part of a team?

We intentionally prefaced each of the three variables, integrity, authenticity, and caring, with the word "perceived." That's because our perceptions are reality for us. Most of us would say we have integrity, but we all know it doesn't do much good to tell someone that – we have to show it and they have to perceive it for themselves. This means learning how team members define integrity, authenticity and caring is essential if we are going to understand their perceptions.

Speaking of showing, Jenny Lucas, Senior Vice President of Operations and Learning at Loews Hotels & Resorts, shared this inspiring story about Loews Corporation that reflected a powerful demonstration of caring for the team. "After Hurricane Katrina, all the team members of our New Orleans property had to immediately leave the city because everything, including the entire coast line, was destroyed, flooded or indefinitely shutdown. Food, drinking water and shelter were scarce. They had no place to stay so some team members even had to go to neighboring states. We were able to get one of our human resource managers from New Orleans to New York City where he figured out where each team member had gone and got them a much-needed paycheck. We continued to pay them while the hotel was closed for repairs, even though many of them weren't working. New Orleans needed an operating hotel as soon as possible to provide accommodations for city rebuilders and people that had lost their homes, and our team members needed their paychecks, even if circumstances meant they couldn't work."

THE TRUST CONTINUUM

Simon Turner, the President of Development for Starwood Hotels and Resorts, previously worked with a group that advised Prince Al-Waleed bin Talal, a member of the royal family of Saudi Arabia. Simon shared with us that the culture of the relationship was shaped by the simple but profound words the prince once said: "Trust is earned. It is not given."

Thomas Glasmacher, the Project Director for the Facility for Rare Isotope Beams at Michigan State University (more on that in Chapter 7) described one important aspect of trust perceptions when he told us how, "Surprises kill trust. Ten percent of a job is written down in the position description, but there's ninety percent which is about context and a shared understanding that is built between the supervisor and the employee. When that shared perception is broken, surprises happen that kill trust."

Since trust must be earned it can also be lost. In other words, trust is dynamic. The Trust Continuum below is one way to visualize this:

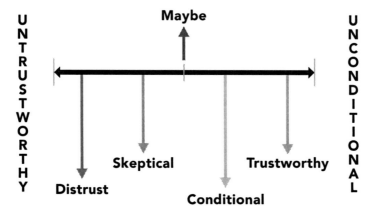

When we meet someone for the first time most of us start off somewhere near the middle, which could be called the "Maybe" point. When we're here we haven't had enough time to perceive someone's integrity, authenticity and level of caring to make a decisive determination.

However, we're busy gathering information. It's a well-known fact that first impressions are formed within seven seconds of meeting someone, so the clock starts ticking right away. We observe until we find a pattern that causes us to move up or down the Trust Continuum. Using the continuum, one story we heard illustrates how trust can be gained and lost rather quickly.

On her first day in her new job leading a team Sarah had individual meetings with each team member and had an overall positive reaction to each one. You could say she moved a little to the right of "Maybe" on the continuum. Two weeks went by and Sarah felt she was really connecting with the team. At that point, one of Sarah's peers stopped her in the hallway and made a comment that absolutely threw her. The colleague told Sarah that she should be careful with what she said to one of her team members, Jason.

In her now heightened state of awareness of Jason's behavior, she observed him making comments over the next couple weeks that put a negative light on the actions of others. Her perception of Jason moved to the left and she became "Skeptical" (doubtful). Eight months passed by with positive interactions with Jason, including a few potentially emotionally challenging conversations that went well. Sarah found herself doubting her previous concerns about Jason and thought she'd been overly influenced by the comment she heard from her colleague. Her trust with Jason moved to the right on the continuum to a "Conditional" level (trust with distinct boundaries).

Imagine Sarah's surprise and disappointment when she was copied on an email thread from someone in which Jason had written a number of derogatory comments about Sarah's work. In that moment her level of trust with Jason moved all the way down to "Distrust" (I have to put energy into protecting myself). When you reach this point, it's very difficult to rebuild trust as a value has most likely been violated. From there, as that pattern gets repeated, the quality of the relationship easily plummets to "Untrustworthy" (not capable of trust). We seriously question whether it is possible to recover from Untrustworthy. Best case, we've seen team members move back to "skeptical" but the doubt never really goes away.

If, on the other hand, Jason's behavior would have continued to be trust-building, the relationship could have moved further to the right and reached the place where the trust level between team members needs to be, which is "Trustworthy" (the pattern of doing what you said is so strong there is little need to check up). It is here, at trust-worthy, that team synergy begins.

Unconditional trust (blind trust) is usually reserved for deeply personal relationships. This is not the level team members need to reach to achieve synergy toward a common goal. In a high-performance team, a strong level of trustworthiness is what's needed.

Please note: in the above example, we commented on Jason's behavior, not his words or his intent. Integrity, authenticity and caring between team members must be demonstrated in actions before trust can be built and continue in a consistent pattern for trust to be maintained.

IMPACT OF BEHAVIOR PATTERNS

As mentioned earlier, we have done extensive work in the area of behavior patterns (a person's regularly repeated actions), which have a significant impact on perceptions of integrity, authenticity and caring. In the previous example, Sarah's belief in Jason's caring about her was deeply shaken by his behavior, which resulted in a breakdown in perceptions of his integrity and authenticity. While it's true that some people may lack these characteristics, we find these breakdowns in perception are often a result of behavior pattern-related challenges.

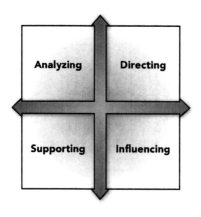

For example, Nicole and Claris have worked together for a few years. Nicole has an Influencing behavior pattern preference, and tends to be highly verbal and emotionally demonstrative. She typically makes decisions quickly and is considered by many to be "the life of the party". Claris has an Analyzing preference, which means she tends to be private and very careful with her words and decisions. Over the years Nicole's verbal, demonstrative behavior has landed on Claris as disingenuous, shallow and ego-centric. To Nicole, Claris's private, cautious behavior seems insecure, critical and stuck-up. Both of their perceptions are based not on their respective intent, but the impact their different behavior patterns make on each other. These types of behavior pattern differences don't always result in a negative impact, but when they do, trust is diminished.

The bottom line here is that on a Team That Works, team members are continually demonstrating behaviors that move levels of trust toward the right on the Trust Continuum. And when there's an erosion of trust it's identified and worked through immediately.

KEY POINTS – HIGH LEVEL OF TRUST

Trust ties into the chemistry part of the relationship. Trust means I am ***willing to be open*** to you. This does not mean I need or am expected to share things about my personal life, but it does mean I am willing to share my knowledge, talents, skills and experience with you for the benefit of the team and team members.

Three things must be present before I will be ***willing to be open*** to you:

1. **A perceived integrity.** You play by rules around courtesy, professionalism and respectful treatment. It is about doing the right thing for me, for the team and for the organization.

2. **A perceived authenticity.** What I see is what I get. You are experienced as real and genuine. There is a pattern to your behavior that allows for predictability so I am not surprised or hurt.

3. **A belief that you care.** I believe you care about me, the team and getting results.

QUESTIONS ABOUT TRUST

Trust is tied closely to values. Upon what values are the team's decisions and actions based? How is this demonstrated?

_____

_____

_____

How do team members define integrity?

_____

_____

_____

When a team member doesn't do what he/she says they will do what is the protocol for addressing it?

_____

_____

_____

What actions demonstrate caring to you? What impact does that have on your willingness to be open?

_____

_____

_____

How do you define honesty? What do you do when you believe someone is not being honest?

_____

_____

_____

CHAPTER THREE

High Level of Respect

Like the roots of an old maple twisted and intertwined under the earth, trust and respect are deeply rooted together. While there is a clear distinction between the two, the symbiotic connection is what grounds a company's culture.

That being said, before diving into this characteristic let's clarify the difference. Even though treating others respectfully is the right thing to do, that's not what this characteristic is about. A high level of respect in the Teams That Work model focuses on the skills and abilities team members have to do their work. In the Task/People yin-yang model we looked at in Chapter 1, trust relates to the People side, while respect relates more to the Task side.

Practically speaking, a high level of respect means all team members have a high regard for each other's skills and abilities to accomplish tasks. Like trust, respect is something that is earned because it comes from the perception of other team members. This aspect of trust was described in our conversation with Burton "Skip" Sack, Past Chair of the National Restaurant Association and former Executive Vice President of Applebee's International. When describing a leader he once worked for Skip said, "He demanded respect, but didn't earn it." This simple flaw – not understanding the source of respect – clearly impacted the effectiveness of the team.

ON THE ROAD AGAIN

Since hospitality is an industry where the whole purpose is to do whatever it takes to make a guest feel welcomed, can you imagine what it was like to stay in a hotel during biblical times? Stories are amassed of people traveling hundreds of miles by foot or by a four-legged form of transportation, always needing to stop for the night. Obviously, there wasn't an app for that, but there is evidence of hotel management dating back to those historic times.

The Greeks offered thermal baths designed for rest and recuperation. Later, the Romans built mansions to provide accommodation for travelers on government business. The Romans were the first to develop thermal baths in England, Switzerland and the Middle East for their guests to use. And that's hospitality 101.

With that in mind, it's not much of a stretch to imagine why the first school for hoteliers was founded in Lausanne, Switzerland in the late 1800s. At the turn of the century the business of hospitality arrived in the U.S. by way of one Mr. Ellsworth M. Statler. Ellsworth had made a great fortune as a hotelier and endowed part of that fortune to start the Cornell University School of Hospitality program (more on that in Chapter 4).

It turned out that, Laurence and Preston Tisch, who built Loews Corporation into what it is today, utilized the good work of Ellsworth Statler to establish the highest standards of customer service anchored in respect. A few years ago, when we started working with Loews, we got to see its culture in motion.

In his book, *The Power of We: Succeeding Through Partnerships*, Jonathan Tisch, Co-chairman of the Board of Loews Corporation and Chairman of Loews Hotels & Resorts, tells the story about how the company got started. "The Tisch family business began in 1935, when my grandfather Al Tisch, who ran a clothing company on New York's Union Square, decided to buy a couple of kids' camps in the Kittatinny Mountains of New Jersey. For the next few years, Al and his wife Sayde ran the camps with the help of their two sons, Laurence and Preston Robert (better known as Larry and Bob). Everybody pitched in, whether running the canteen, waiting on tables in the dining hall or picking up campers at the train station. That style of a working partnership became a family tradition – one that persists to this day."

This notion of "partnership" the Tisch family exemplified includes teamwork where respect is demonstrated by delegating authority and responsibility. It continues to be a hallmark of what was to become the Loews Corporation. In 1946, Bob and Larry saw a local advertisement indicating the Laurel-in-the-Pines hotel was up for lease. They figured running a hotel couldn't be harder than running a summer camp, so they purchased the lease. They found their wide breadth of experience in operations, finance and customer service made them pretty good at this hotel management thing. Their hard work and business savvy paid off in spades and in two short years, the hotel was profitable. This success paved the way for them to build another hotel to the tune of $17 million dollars in 1956. In the first year of its operation that hotel generated $12 million. How does that happen? By making smart operational decisions and anchoring the culture in respect.

More than 50 years later, when we talked with various leaders at Loews Corporation, we saw how respect flows fluidly as part of the company's DNA. It's not surprising given how deeply imbedded it was in the founding of the company.

Jonathan Tisch, Bob Tisch's son, still talks about the company's roots with family pride. "Loews is large and diverse, but the values we learned from my father and uncle are still present every day. Even as Loews Hotels has grown into the Loews Corporation with four distinct businesses, Bob and Larry's values continue to be the foundation on which we base every decision."

Andrew Tisch, Larry's son and Co-chairman of the Board and Chairman of the Executive Committee of Loews Corporation, told us how "Bob and Larry served as role models of what respect looks like during their 55 years as business partners. They demonstrated and emphasized the importance of respecting the skills and abilities of everyone they hired."

ROOTED IN RESPECT

Alan Momeyer, the Vice President of Human Resources for Loews Corporation showed us how Bob and Larry engendered respect in everyone they hired.

"Back in 1980, about six months after I started working for Loews Theatres, I walked into Bob's office where he, Larry and the President of Loews Theatres were sitting around the conference table talking. They had an idea about putting a first-run movie theater in Greenwich Village in New York City on what was a parking lot. However, the Greenwich Village community board was vehemently opposed to it. I suggested a plan to have the IT department provide me a list of all the employees of Loews who lived in Greenwich Village, and then create an initiative with those people on a committee to promote the idea of a new movie theater in their neighborhood. Bob and Larry let me run with it and, not long after, the community board approved the theatre. Even though I was new Bob and Larry respected my idea, which made it clear that's how they did business and how they expected me to do business."

Alan recalled another story that highlighted how rooted respect is in Loews Corporations' culture. "The CFO of our Hotel Company had been with the company for about a month and was attending a meeting with Bob and Larry. They were discussing a business problem and the CFO assumed Bob or Larry would decide how to proceed and direct people accordingly. But in fact, they turned to him and said, 'Do the best you can and let us know how it turns out.' The CFO may have been a deer in the headlights, but this demonstration of respect by Bob and Larry is still a significant building block in Loews culture. Their philosophy is to hire good people and empower them to take responsibility, use their skills and abilities and prove themselves."

DEFINING A HIGH LEVEL OF RESPECT

Like trust, respect is earned; others bestow it on us, not because we request or demand it, but because we demonstrate competence in the work we do.

Since respect has to do with technical competence it also impacts the fifth characteristic in the Teams That Work model: focus on results. When team members have a high regard for each other's skills and abilities to accomplish tasks, results improve. Mark Battle, the head of stamping operations for Fiat Chrysler Automobiles (FCA) Chrysler Group, LLC, responsible for the management of six NAFTA stamping plants, oversees three separate highly specialized areas of expertise that must work together to produce stamping parts for the company. He made the link between respect and results when he told us about an impact the change in leadership at the company in 2007 has had. "Current leadership shows a lot of respect for all three specialized areas of stamping, which is reflected in the performance and quality of our parts. The fit and finish is better and the cost is not out of line. Timing of delivery of tools and parts to the plants is better. We are now very much engaged in world class manufacturing. Respect for our different areas of skill and expertise combined with the ability to work together is absolutely instrumental to these improvements."

RELATIONSHIP BETWEEN TRUST AND RESPECT

Although trust and respect are connected there is an important difference, illustrated by two scenarios that unfolded at a credit union we worked with a few years ago.

In the first scenario, Terry, a five-year employee at the credit union, applied for and was promoted from a front-line customer service position to Director of Member Services. Her boss, Marcus, was the Vice President of Operations and felt that even though this position would be a challenge for Terry, the amount of good will and trust she had engendered with the members over the years would serve her well in the new role.

After a few months Marcus noticed an uptick in the number of member complaints the credit union was receiving and did some research. He found that while no one said anything negative about Terry in their comments, the number of errors made by the member services department had dramatically increased. Marcus isolated three main areas where the errors were made and all of them were directly linked to work Terry had done in the database used to track communications with members. He met with Terry and discussed how use of the system was a critical requirement for her new position. To be successful in the role she needed to master the technology, so they came up with a skill development plan.

However, nine months later Terry's performance in this area was still below the needed level. On top of that, it was taking her twice as long as the benchmark standard to complete the tasks, which didn't leave much time for her to do the parts of the role she most enjoyed.

Marcus realized he'd made a mistake, and that Terry simply did not have the technical aptitude required for the role. Even though she was a trustworthy person, she lacked the ability to do the job. Fortunately, Terry agreed, which made the resolution much easier for everyone.

In the second scenario, Lisa, the Vice President of Sales and Marketing, had an opening for a new director of marketing. The credit union had fallen behind the times on marketing strategy, specifically in the area of social media. One of the candidates she interviewed, Chen, had excellent credentials in social media marketing and so, despite lacking much business experience, Lisa hired him for the position.

Within six months Chen's efforts had created a 2.7 percent market increase, which was a remarkable achievement considering the size of the credit union and the competition's footprint in the space. However, two of Chen's direct reports had quit during that time, citing his "unprofessional" behavior as the primary reason for their leaving. Lisa also heard from Marcus that the grapevine was full of stories about how Chen had offended some of his colleagues. Lisa had never experienced this with Chen, so she decided to have a conversation with him to see what she could uncover. Not surprisingly, Chen denied any wrongdoing and felt the rumors were coming from someone internal who applied for but was not hired for his position. Lisa was uneasy about the outcome of the meeting but decided to give Chen the benefit of the doubt.

One month later at a joint meeting of both the sales and marketing teams, Lisa observed Chen treating the two members of his team whom he'd hired noticeably differently than those who had been in place prior to his employment. When she tried to discuss what she'd observed with him in their 1:1 meeting the following week, he became very quiet, and again, denied any wrongdoing. The next day HR notified Lisa that Chen had filed a formal complaint of workplace harassment against her. After an ugly month of mediation Chen was terminated from the position. Unfortunately, another six months of litigation followed before the situation was fully resolved.

Situations like the ones Marcus and Lisa faced with Terry and Chen don't frequently follow a nice, clean path to resolution. Most often, they are fraught with emotional turmoil and difficult conversations. Yet some variation of these scenarios is common in the workplace. In the situation with Terry, respect was the issue, while in Chen's situation trust was the core problem.

When levels of trust or respect are low it makes it impossible for a team to work together, let alone perform at a high level. Energy is lost to making sure that teammates are doing what they said they would do and are meeting the standard the team agreed to. The energy it takes to get the work done is dissipated as their effort goes into overseeing, correcting and fixing the problem.

However, when both trust and respect are in place, team members take responsibility. They do what they say they are going to do and meet or exceed the standards set. Reliability is clearly present and the resulting synergy increases productivity, profitability and quality. The team's energy is directed into accomplishing the goal and everyone gains respect and credibility.

The challenge is understanding that trust and respect are not goals to be achieved, or objectives to be attained. Trust and respect are the outcomes of working together effectively.

Stephen Cummings, General Manager for Loews Don Cesar in St. Pete Beach, Florida, summed up the point of these stories with this statement: "To be successful, you can't be *either* trustworthy or skilled; you must be both."

We couldn't agree more.

TRUST, RESPECT AND BEHAVIOR PATTERNS

Before we close this chapter on respect, we'd like to take a few minutes to revisit the subject of behavior patterns because, as we mentioned earlier, the first two characteristics in the Teams That Work model are often the most heavily impacted by this variable. Let's consider four members of an executive team we recently worked with: Bianca, Abdul, Evan and Jacqueline.

Bianca, the CFO, was known for her quiet, reserved nature and attention to detail, both of which were reflected in her analyzing behavior pattern preference.

Abdul, VP of Sales, was a highly social and energetic person that was very comfortable in front of groups, which was reflected in his influencing preference.

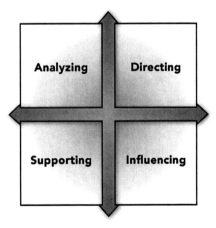

Evan was CTO and wanted things done as quickly as possible, which was reflected in his directing pattern preference.

Jacqueline, the CEO, had an amazing knack for being able to balance the ability to drive for results and making tough decisions while demonstrating support for her team. Her behavior pattern preference was both directing and supporting, an unusual combination given the strong contrast of these two markedly different patterns.

Although Jacqueline's team performed at a fairly high level, she knew there were some less-than-ideal dynamics under the surface. In their weekly 1:1s, Bianca had expressed her frustration to Jacqueline over the incomplete information she felt Abdul provided. As a result, she kept putting more policies into place to try to change things.

On more than one occasion Evan, the CTO, mentioned his concern that Bianca wasn't tough enough in negotiating the best price from vendors. Bianca found out Evan had gone around her once to try to get a better deal on something and, understandably, things had been tense between them ever since.

There was also a less-than-open relationship between Abdul and Evan because Evan heard that Abdul had called him" cold-blooded" behind his back. When asked about it, Abdul said he had meant it as a compliment, but that didn't help matters.

All of these challenges had a negative impact on the levels of trust and respect between the members of Jacqueline's team, and ultimately impacted productivity and the team's performance. As a consequence, the direct and difficult conversations (more on this in Chapter 5) that were necessary to resolve these situations were now avoided.

Numerous things can impact trust and respect but in working with this team we discovered all of these challenges to trust and respect were directly related to negative impacts from the different behavior pattern preferences of team members. Once the team recognized this and learned how to work more effectively with these differences, levels of trust and respect improved.

KEY POINTS – HIGH LEVEL OF RESPECT

Respect ties into the talents, skills and abilities that an individual brings to the team. It is linked to the fact that you are good at doing something. I have a high *regard* for your ability to use your talent and skills.

Although trust and respect are related, they are not the same thing. Someone may be a trustworthy person, but not technically skilled for the job they have been hired to do. Or an individual may be technically brilliant but untrustworthy.

Also, trust and respect don't happen easily or automatically. Trust and respect are earned over time when you work together on a task. When both trust and respect are present, team members have what they need to truly *rely on* each other.

QUESTIONS ABOUT RESPECT

What talents and skills (technical, strategic, interpersonal, etc.) do you hold in high regard?

_____

_____

_____

Are the talents and skills you identified in #1 the same that other people see when they work with you? What are the variables that impact this?

_____

_____

_____

How does respect impact the level of engagement team members have with each other? What actions demonstrate engagement?

_____

_____

_____

In what way does respect from others (or perceived lack of respect) impact your team's performance?

_____

_____

_____

What types of opportunities exist for team members to provide input on team decisions, and how are these handled?

_____

_____

_____

CHAPTER FOUR

Commitment to a Clear and Common Purpose

The human genome consists of 3 billion letters written in a cryptic four-letter code. Even if you read three letters of the code per second 24 hours a day it would still take 31 years to complete it. It's no wonder the Human Genome Project is known as the largest collaborative biological project in the history of the world. Using 20 universities and research centers in the United States, the United Kingdom, Japan, France, Germany and China, a team of scientists from around the world took 13 years to determine the sequence of these 3 billion letters.

The project is arguably the most well-known example of commitment to a clear and common purpose in the last two decades. Persistent effort grounded in commitment to the goal, resulted in what is now considered the most significant scientific advancement in health sciences in modern history and the best example of multi-year transnational teamwork ever imagined.

While there are thousands of examples of teams with a clear and common purpose achieving stunning success, we found a remarkable example of this thread of commitment in an organization with a long legacy. Our client, Cornell University School of Hotel Administration, has been the preeminent school for hospitality management education for more than nine decades.

LIFE IS SERVICE

In Chapter 3 we discussed hotelier Ellsworth Statler, who founded the largest hotel chain of his day. He believed that "Life is service – the one who progresses is the one who gives his fellow men a little more – a little better service." This clarity of purpose served him well in the hospitality industry. A self-made millionaire, Ellsworth was invited to attend the Hotel Ezra Cornell conference in 1927.

Before the conference Ellsworth was a strong skeptic about the idea of classroom learning for a career in hospitality, but something unexpected happened. As Brad Edmondson, author of *Hospitality Leadership: The Cornell Hotel School*, describes it, "Statler took a day-long tour of Cornell's facilities during the conference, and saw that the instructors had the same spirit of experimentation, questioning and innovation that had helped him become successful. He recognized the positive impact this approach could have on developing hospitality skills and, shortly after that tour, became the school's greatest benefactor." This shift in his thinking caused him to make a contribution that helped set Cornell on its way to becoming the world's foremost hospitality management program.

Cornell University's School of Hotel Administration was the first collegiate program in hospitality management and is regarded today as the world leader in its field. Since its inception, its mission was simple: To develop leaders for the hospitality industry. It's evolved over time, but what has stayed constant is its strong commitment and clarity of purpose. Many extraordinary leaders in the hospitality industry are Cornell alums, including Lee Pillsbury, Chairman and CEO of Thayer Lodging Group, Burton "Skip" Sack, Past Chair of the National Restaurant Association and former Executive Vice President of Applebee's International, Ted Teng, President and CEO of The Leading Hotels of the World, Ltd., Simon Turner, President of Starwood International and Andrew Tisch, Co-chairman of the Board and Chairman of the Executive Committee of Loews Corporation. The school has also had a tremendous impact on and received support from many other leaders in the industry we spoke with, including John Ceriale, President of Prospect Advisors, the exclusive hotel advisor to Blackstone Real Estate.

Along with these individuals, we were fortunate to talk with faculty and staff members Nancy Weislogel, the Executive Director of Online Learning and Collaborative Programs at the hotel school, Bill Carroll, Clinical Professor of Marketing, Jan deRoos, Associate Professor and HVS (Hotel Valuation Services) Professor of Hotel Finance and Real Estate, and Emily Franco, Director of the School of Hotel Administration and The Culinary Institute of America Alliance. Although each of these individuals provided different stories and perspectives, they all shared a strong connection to Ellsworth's belief manifested in the work of the school. In fact, we learned of Ellsworth's "Life is service..." quote from Lee Pillsbury. Lee vividly remembers seeing the quote on the wall at the school and told us how that quote was part of what made "the hotel school a career experience and not just a school experience".

GAINING COMMITMENT

When team members are committed to a clear and common purpose it means they are "all in". Another way of saying this is, "there are no excuses". As you can imagine, reaching this level of commitment is not easy. To understand this characteristic, it's essential to break it down to its individual elements.

First, why do we use the word purpose? What we're after here is the core reason the team exists. Honest discussion centered around what the team does practically creates a meaningful purpose statement that can elicit the all in commitment.

Nancy Weislogel drove home the importance of commitment when she described the purpose of the Online Learning and Collaborative Programs department. "We offer 50 individual online courses and 15 certificate tracks. In a given year people from 200 countries buy 20,000 courses. We can't do all this work without clarity of and commitment to our purpose. We sink or swim together."

She's right, but getting to a clear and common level of clarity takes work, and there are challenges.

1. It could be clear but not common (Everyone has the same understanding of what needs to be done, but one or more members don't want to do it and are not going to do it).

2. It could be common but not clear (We all want to do it but we have different understandings of what "it" is).

If all team members do not have clarity, and don't know that others have the same clarity, by nature it cannot be a clear and common purpose. Stephen Cummings from Loews Hotels commented, "A clear and common purpose is not negotiable. It *is* or it is not". The power of shared clarity is essential for everyone to reach full commitment level to a team's purpose.

Additionally, three characteristics are needed to reach full commitment:

1. Larger Than Self

    The purpose of the team needs to be larger than self. Although there are self-serving and narcissistic individuals, nearly everyone wants to make a positive difference in the world. Teams that allow an individual to become larger or more important than the team lose full commitment of all team members. In these cases you hear statements like, "I am going to do this and this. You people do whatever you want".

It's true that some teams exist to help one person (such as a political candidate campaign), but even in these cases there is a perception of some type of "higher order" benefit or purpose. In this instance, the candidate is making a difference on issues the team members' support. This in turn inspires the team members to make a commitment.

2. WIIFM

There needs to be enough of a clear W-I-I-F-M, (What's-In-It-For-Me) for each member of the team to be all in. Even though the purpose of the team has to be larger than any one individual, every member needs to perceive there's a benefit for them. Even teams that give themselves for an altruistic cause do so because at some point each person on the team came to the belief that the cause was worth supporting for their own benefit as well.

At the core, when the WIIFM for each team member is strong enough for them to make a commitment to a common purpose, there tends to be an alignment with personal values. Mark Emmert, President of the NCAA, highlighted this point when he told us, "The NCAA continually stays focused on our core values. Our values are the undergirding for the purpose of everything we do. Things become extremely difficult when there are conflicting values. When it is your son or daughter, your school or your conference, different perceptions of the same value emerge. The singular focus on the common purpose aligned with values is imperative". Interestingly enough, this struggle to align common purpose and values creates the need for the third characteristic.

3. Room For Disagreement

When a team is creating its purpose there needs to be room for disagreement. In other words, if a clear and common purpose has not already been established, there must be room for conversation, discussion and disagreement. Each team member needs to believe that his or her voice is heard. The critical issue is not that the final purpose was exactly what an individual wanted, but that everyone felt they had the opportunity to influence the common purpose. Individuals who believe or feel they could not influence the common purpose will not be able to genuinely commit. There will be a hesitancy or doubt in their actions or voice, and this hesitancy in behavior will eventually impact the trust level within the group.

Jenny Lucas from Loews Hotel reinforced this point when she shared a story about reexamining service standards at hotels. "I was at a meeting and we were discussing what happens at all the touch points, such as what do you do when someone calls customer service. It was a healthy conversation, with lots of disagreement and passionate debate. In the end the group reached a higher level of commitment because everyone had a voice and their voice was heard."

One of our consultants worked with a team of eight people who struggled for a couple of hours to create a clear and common purpose statement. When the statement was finally written on the board, the consultant had everyone pick up a packet of sticky notes. He said that after all the work they had done it would be easy to make the mistake of assuming the clear and common purpose was enough, but commitment had not yet been confirmed. So he asked them to toss their packets into a circle in the middle of the table if they were willing to fully commit to the purpose they had created.

Imagine the surprise on the team when one member held back. That act started an additional 10 minute conversation that resulted in a slight alteration to the statement. When the consultant asked for commitment the second time all the team members willingly tossed their packet into the circle. This team member had fully participated in the two-hour discussion, but something held her back when the moment of decision came. Room for disagreement allowed everyone on the team to get to full commitment, and most importantly, commitment wasn't assumed just because the purpose was clear and common.

Healthy, respectful conversations about a common purpose that is aligned with values and has room for discussion and disagreement leads to commitment, the kind of commitment where responsible behavior shows up every day.

FROM COMMITMENT TO COLLABORATION

One of the benefits of having commitment to a clear and common purpose is how it encourages collaboration. Bill Carroll, who we introduced earlier in the chapter, teaches revenue management, economics, pricing, yield management and new media (quantitative aspects of marketing) at Cornell. He shared how the alumni of the School of Hotel Administration stay involved and about the high level of collaboration between professors and alumni. Bill explained that he's "seen collaboration in many areas, including the development of the mission, vision and values statement, with the participation of the faculty. This type of collaboration happens because of the strong commitment these individuals have to the mission of the school".

Alan Whitted, the global head of Press Shops and Dies for Fiat Chrysler Automobiles (FCA), is responsible for global stamping engineering and die manufacturing. Alan told us about the extraordinary results the team has achieved for the past six years. He explained that this level of performance "required new levels of collaboration between Manufacturing, Engineering, Quality, Operations, Procurement, Finance and Human Resources. These different parts of the organization had to work together with a clear and common purpose, delivering a consistent message for us to achieve what we've achieved".

In Chapter 3 we mentioned Jonathan Tisch's book, *The Power of We: Succeeding Through Partnerships*. Jonathan writes, "It's a simple philosophy based on putting aside our individual concerns in order to work together toward a greater good." This is what a team does when they follow these guidelines and commits to a clear and common purpose. Without it collaboration will be mostly superficial. Furthermore, a lack of a common purpose creates a pathway for doubt. When doubt appears, energy moves from accomplishing the common purpose and problem solving to protecting and defending individual goals or "my perception" of the purpose. As the protecting and defending grows, silos emerge and collaboration moves from the common purpose to protecting a silo.

REMOVING THE SILOS

An example of the challenges of silos took place with a consulting firm we worked with a few years ago.

When the company was founded their focus was on project management services, and over the years they created a stellar regional reputation. The President and the Board felt it would be a good idea to expand the services the company offered, so they made a friendly acquisition of a well-established strategic planning consulting practice. They did the same with an IT consulting business. Two years later the President retired and an external candidate was selected to take his place. It was just a few months after that change when we were contacted by Jennifer, the new President, to help her work through some challenges she was having with her leadership team.

When we interviewed the individuals on the team it was apparent that even though the acquisitions were friendly, they had not been without bumps and bruises. As a result, three silos with three distinct cultures had formed within the company, which was trying to operate as a single business entity.

The previous vice president of the project management business had retired a year earlier and the new vice president, Derrick, had been with the company since its inception. Derrick was very well connected with the business community and it was no secret that the success and reputation of the project management company was largely due to his bigger-than-life personality. In every word and action, Derrick lived the purpose of the project management side of the business.

The Vice President of Strategic Planning, Ron, had been retained through the acquisition and was determined to make sure they did not become an afterthought. He was concerned that the acquisition of the IT business was taking energy and time away from the development of his side of the business. Ron felt that the mission statement of the strategic planning line had always been strong and saw no reason to change his thinking.

Finally, there was Sharon, Founder and President of the IT consulting business before the acquisition who was now the vice president. Although her line of business was currently the smallest, she felt it gave the larger company a much higher level of relevance and credibility. She agreed to the acquisition because she believed that it would give her business quick visibility and scalability. With that, she was confident the IT business would outgrow the other lines of business within a few years and was determined to see that happen.

Although each of these individuals was highly talented and skilled, they each had their own agendas and those agendas were not aligned. Jennifer was aware of the tension that existed between the three lines of business but felt that the tension was necessary and helpful. That line of thinking may have been true if the three lines were aligned. Unfortunately, the tension between the three VPs was pulling the company apart. The foundation required for the team to move out of silos into collaboration was missing.

For the next three months, we conducted numerous meetings and did extensive work, finally arriving at a clear joint purpose. It still took another year for it to become reality but the company's foundation was significantly strengthened. In the process, Sharon was given a severance and left the company, Ron was nearly terminated at one point. Derrick strongly considered returning to his previous position and a couple of board members expressed the opinion that Jennifer was the wrong person for the job. Fortunately, Jennifer knew the only way for the company to reach true collaboration would be if the executive team fully bought into the purpose, and she refused to bend on that expectation. She recognized that unless the senior leaders talked and acted in a way that modeled a united culture the silos would remain.

Once she knew the new united culture was established at the top, she encouraged the team leaders of the three lines of business to create their own purpose statements, making sure they aligned with the larger purpose of the company.

Establishing a commitment to a clear and common purpose where team members have the opportunity to influence creates the foundation for a Team That Works. It becomes the cornerstone on which all actions align and creates true collaboration while preventing splintering and silos from forming within the team.

KEY POINTS – COMMITMENT TO A CLEAR AND COMMON PURPOSE

When team members are fully invested in a goal that everyone understands, they are *all in* on the purpose.

- We use the word **Clear** to eliminate misunderstandings. Misunderstandings occur when everyone uses the same words, but the words don't mean the same thing. "Take care of it" does not mean the same thing to everyone. We have to be clear in our communication or team members can't be sure what the expectations are.

- We use the word **Common** to make sure everyone is on the same page. We need to agree on the priority, the resources and the urgency.

- We use the word **Purpose** because it is "higher order" than a goal. Achieving the purpose is fulfilling the larger intent, while completing a goal is simply accomplishing the task (e.g., the purpose is to attract and retain world class talent; the goal is to expand our selection process outside the region.)

It is one thing to make something **Clear** and quite another to have it be **Common**. Clarity by itself gets **interest**: "I will do it if it is convenient." **All in** is about commitment – there are no excuses, only results. Three elements are needed to reach this level:

1. Discussion about and connection to something that is larger than self.

2. There's something in it for me – personal integrity, belonging to something larger than me, achievement of the goal, making a difference.

3. There's room for disagreement. The discussion and resolution of disagreement begets the clarity that is the cornerstone of trust and respect.

A commitment to a clear and common purpose creates true collaboration while preventing splintering and silos from forming within the team.

QUESTIONS ABOUT PURPOSE

What is the team's purpose? How do you know the purpose is clear to all team members?

_____

_____

_____

To what degree is the purpose of the team reflected in the behaviors and actions of the team?

_____

_____

_____

How much are team members willing to personally risk for the purpose to become reality?

_____

_____

_____

In what way do your values align (or not align) with the team's purpose?

_____

_____

_____

How do your priorities align (or not align) with the team's purpose? How do the other team members' priorities align (or not align) with the purpose? What needs to happen to align everyone's priorities?

_____

_____

_____

CHAPTER FIVE

Willingness and Ability to Manage Conflict

When people work together disagreements are inevitable. If you are married, in a relationship, or simply related to someone – anyone – you've experienced conflict. Sure, it can be uncomfortable, even painful. But conflict is unavoidable. And the key to conflict is how it's managed. That's what determines how successful those relationships will be.

Misunderstandings, unmet expectations, a values violation – whatever the cause, conflict can be a source of great difficulty. But when team members know how to engage in difficult conversations, conflict reduces uncertainty and provides opportunities for teams to gain clarity and improve performance.

Due in great part to its role, one of our clients; the National Collegiate Athletic Association (NCAA) is no stranger to conflict. One of their responsibilities is governance, and given that they must deal with college-level athletes, it comes with the territory. As a result, the NCAA has a wealth of experience with organizational conflict, and regularly manages some highly controversial and very public disagreements.

COLLEGE FOOTBALL ALMOST WENT AWAY

The NCAA formed during Theodore Roosevelt's presidency. In fact, it was a result of trying to cut college football altogether because of repeated injuries and deaths on the fields of colleges and universities across the nation. In the early 20th century, the President convened two White House conferences to "encourage reforms" or discontinue the sport. On December 28, 1905 in New York, 62 higher-education institutions became charter members of the Intercollegiate Athletic Association of the United States (IAAUS). The IAAUS was officially established on March 31, 1906, and took its present name, the NCAA, in 1910.

Since then, the NCAA has evolved significantly, but two dominant attributes have remained consistent:

1. It is an association that currently includes more than 1,100 member schools – responsible for regulatory functions (i.e., governance model), and a service provider, particularly services that support and run 89 National Championships.

2. It is democratic – policy decisions are made by the member schools with the NCAA President acting as the de facto spokesperson, moderator and leader.

Since 2010, Mark Emmert has served as President of the NCAA. With more than 30 years of experience managing the lives of student athletes and public policy around higher education, including five years as Chancellor of Louisiana State University (LSU) and six years as the President of the University of Washington, Mark has an extensive background with the various dynamics involved in college athletics. A key requirement for this position is to have a depth of knowledge and experience dealing with intercollegiate athletics and academic issues – including practice with strategic conflict management skills.

DIFFICULT DECISIONS

By the nature of being an association with so many member schools of different sizes, needs and expectations, the NCAA is frequently involved in conflict. As Mark explained, "The NCAA is very much a democratic, representative model, because all of the decisions that are made around policy and regulatory functions are made by the members themselves and not by me or the staff here. My job is less like the commissioner of the NFL or NBA and more like the Secretary General of the United Nations. The differences between a small liberal-arts college and a large research university is a bit like the differences between Ghana and China. Both of these countries are members of the United Nations but their interest couldn't be more different."

In 2011, one university found itself in the center of a national media firestorm. When the Penn State scandal broke involving its football team, the NCAA, by its regulatory design, played a significant role. When we spoke with Mark he told us the scandal was a "deeply disturbing incident, shockingly disruptive to a great university, that forced the executive committee (a group of university presidents), to make some very difficult decisions regarding Penn State." Without delving into the well-documented public details of the scandal, it is a clear example of intense conflict, arguably one of the most high-profile conflicts the NCAA has faced. But it certainly isn't the only difficult situation they have dealt with.

Working through difficult situations with member institutions is a common practice for regulatory agencies, and this is an important aspect of the work of the NCAA. Since it is not a completely independent agency, the NCAA has nothing to do with the removal of the coaches, the criminal investigations or the investigations at Penn State. After those events occurred, the NCAA acted in the face of the "awful facts and deeply emotional issues" which existed separate from the very public actions taken by other institutions.

LESSONS LEARNED

Although few teams have to deal with the intensity of a situation like the NCAA faced with Penn State, there are lessons to be learned from how it was handled:

1. **Core values serve as a compass to guide the conversations.** The NCAA helped refocus Penn State on its core values. This is extremely important because when values are violated strong emotions tend to cloud logic, facts and data.

2. **Continue to support each other's dignity.** To maintain trust after experiencing conflict, team members needed to support each other's dignity. For this to happen, common responses such as blaming, withdrawing, attacking, placating, criticizing and ignoring needed to be replaced with actions that demonstrate support and integrity. This doesn't mean there isn't responsibility or consequences for actions, but giving each other a way to process the conflict while maintaining dignity is critical. It means staying forward-focused and solving problems instead of fixing blame. Conflict-related conversations should clarify the difference between what was agreed to related to common purpose and core values, and what actually happened.

3. **Focus on desired outcomes.** In the Penn State scandal the NCAA crafted, for the first time, an athletic integrity agreement similar to corporate integrity agreements that had been used in private companies. The goal was to help Penn State make necessary changes and get on the road to recovery as quickly as possible. Similarly, in conflict it's critical for team

conversations to be focused on problem solving and improvement, not defending, blaming or protecting. This doesn't mean there can't be consequences for some actions, but the consequences are aligned with the desired outcomes.

4. **Acknowledge and affirm.** The NCAA affirmed the work of Penn State for their exemplary implementation of the agreement. When teams respond well to conflict and take action on the agreements that are reached, it's important for team members to acknowledge and affirm that work. This type of recognition and ownership can strengthen a team's identity.

Let's turn our attention from the NCAA and Penn State story to the practical definition of conflict and what teams need to do to capitalize on it.

WILLING AND ABLE

A practical definition of this characteristic is that team members ask the difficult questions and address the issues. In other words, they mitigate the "elephants in the room" or the issues people are aware of but afraid to mention. As you can imagine, this is much easier said than done, which is why we use both the words "willing and able". Some people are willing to address issues but aren't skilled at it. Others may be skilled at asking difficult questions but, because of low levels of trust, aren't willing to do it. Both the ability (skill) and willingness (trust based on support) are necessary if team members are going to ask the difficult questions.

And most importantly, the environment needs to be safe – or frankly, all bets are off. If team members feel they will be criticized or their positions threatened if they address issues directly, they will remain silent. If difficult conversations are encouraged and supported, people will feel safe to say what would otherwise be hidden from view.

As we pointed out earlier, conflict is an inevitable part of people working together. You've probably heard the term "fight or flight". This refers to the common reactions people have when facing conflict. By choosing "flight", they avoid, placate, ignore, pacify, etc. By choosing "fight", they attack, blame, criticize, accuse, etc. While these responses are natural and sometimes appropriate, they do not create positive outcomes in the workplace.

Fight and flight responses are survival-based, and trigger strong physiological changes in the human body. In these modes people demonstrate reactive behavior that is focused on short-term decisions using only the information on hand. (Think: There's a bear. Run!) High-performance teams learn how to work with conflict in a way that benefits their performance. (Think: There's a bear. Don't run! Quickly analyze and practice what works.) So the goal is not to eliminate conflict, but to manage it to the team's advantage.

In one of our interviews, Skip Sack, former Executive Vice President of Applebee's International, relayed a story about how he made asking difficult questions a regular part of the workplace. "In order for the teams in my franchises to run more effectively, I held regular weekly meetings with our employees. No managers or regional supervisors were present – not even the VP of operations. It was just me and the CFO, and we asked three simple, direct questions:

1. What are we doing that we should stop doing?

2. What are we doing that we should change?

3. What are we not doing that we should be doing?"

Sometimes when employees give honest answers to these types of questions, the information can be hard to hear. But that's what starts difficult conversations. The answers to these questions are precisely the ones that help teams and organizations improve. Without this level of honesty the truth simply gets buried.

THE TRUST FACTOR

In Chapter 2, we looked at the variables for building trust, which impacts willingness. Many team members tell us they are willing, but they don't have the ability or skill. This is where most people need help. This is not surprising given that many people have not had conflict management skills training. Most of us simply use the methods we learned from our families or friends, which, in some form or another, sound a bit like, "Because I said so!", "Leave me alone!" or "What's your problem?" Obviously these techniques don't transfer well into the workplace. If teams are going to manage conflict well, it's important they have strong skills to do it.*

Alan Whitted, the global head of Press & Dies at FCA, told us about a pre-bankruptcy cultural phenomenon that he referred to as "Liar's Poker". Liar's Poker started because the company culture fostered a fear of asking questions and revealing problems. "The mentality was to let other people talk about their problems so they would take the criticism and that would allow you time to fix your own problems without anyone knowing about it." (Recognize the avoidance of conflict in this statement?) "Now, post-bankruptcy, everyone discusses their issues and asks for help from other groups and leadership when they need it. There are regular meetings where people are expected to talk about their progress and any problems they may be having so they can get the proper help in a timely manner. These meetings aren't always easy but the culture is much better than it was with Liar's

Poker. Now, we resolve problems and improve outcomes instead of avoiding real issues and hoping others will fail before you do."

Maintaining trust after experiencing conflict is also critical. The immediate response to conflict is to question the other person's intent (i.e., "Why did they do/say that?"). If the intent cannot be tied to the common purpose and the core values, then negative assumptions are made and the seeds of disintegration are sown. One note of caution: when addressing conflict a common mistake is discussing the "what" happened and "how" it happened, but not clarifying the "why" it happened. The "why" is not about blaming or rationalizing, but is necessary to provide the context and explanation of the cause of the conflict. Once that happens, people can start to move toward the problem-solving mode that's required to reach resolution.

Pradeep and Karen were business partners in a small firm whose decisions had a big impact on each other. Pradeep would often take actions that had a negative impact on Karen without discussing them or even informing her. One example was when Pradeep hired someone without Karen's knowledge. Imagine her surprise when she arrived at the office and met the new hire! When Karen brought this up with Pradeep he would focus the conversation on what he did and how he did it, but avoided discussing why he did it. When Karen would ask questions about why he made the decision without talking with her about it, first Pradeep would get defensive and accuse Karen of not trusting him. "I told you we needed to hire someone for this position. Why don't you believe me?"

After these types of conversations Karen would initially have a sense the conflict had been resolved but something about the unclarified "why" would work its way back into her thoughts and create doubt. Over time these doubts eroded Karen's ability to trust Pradeep, and others in the company were affected because they didn't have clarity about the why.

Bringing up problems increases the potential for conflict and difficult conversations, but it also increases the quality of performance because real problems get addressed and corrected. Thus, learning to navigate conflict is a critical skillset for Teams That Work.

Note: Effectiveness Institute offers a one-day workshop, Navigating Conflict, which provides the skills and tools to manage conflict effectively and keep the focus on the common purpose while honoring values.

KEY POINTS – WILLINGNESS AND ABILITY TO MANAGE CONFLICT

Resolving conflict is a counter-intuitive behavior in our culture. Team members must be willing and able to ***ask the difficult questions*** and address the issues.

If conflict is not addressed, it simply goes underground where it lingers, grows and negatively impedes the development of trust and respect. The challenge is to surface, discuss and resolve conflict so that all energy goes into goal achievement.

There are two tendencies to resolving conflict that are not productive:

- Ignoring the conflict (flight).
- Becoming overly aggressive (fight).

Neither extreme works because they both fail to addresses the issues or feelings underlying the conflict. If the feelings are not addressed and resolved, they fester. These unresolved negative feelings will reappear, usually with greater intensity and with a destructive force. And if the issues are not addressed the team performance suffers.

QUESTIONS ABOUT CONFLICT

In what way does the team create (or not create) an environment of mutual effort and open communication for talking about frustrations or concerns?

_____

_____

_____

Does the team tend to move toward difficult conversations when necessary, or avoid them? Why is that your perception?

_____

_____

_____

If the environment does not seem safe enough for you to ask difficult questions, what needs to change?

_____

_____

_____

How would you rate your skill level at managing conflict effectively? How would you rate your team member's skills?

_____

_____

_____

Having productive difficult conversations requires focusing on a future desired state that fixes problems rather than a past-focused state that leads to defending, justifying and blaming. Where do your team's difficult conversations tend to focus?

_____

_____

_____

CHAPTER SIX

Focus on Results

At the end of the day, this is the characteristic teams are evaluated on, and appropriately so. Why should a team exist if they don't do what they were created to do? But this is about more than the criteria for evaluating performance. Focusing on results is both an action and a mindset.

In 2010 we began working with Fiat Chrysler Automobiles (FCA), which had undergone a major leadership transition three years earlier. A focused reset on results was one of the key variables the new leadership brought to the company that helped generate a stunning turnaround.

SELF MOVERS

Chrysler was founded by Walter Chrysler in 1925, when the Maxwell Motor Company (established in 1904) was reorganized into the Chrysler Corporation. The company was well known for its pioneering practices. Among the innovations in its early years was the first practical mass-produced four-wheel hydraulic brakes system engineered by Chrysler with patents assigned to Lockheed. Chrysler pioneered rubber engine mounts to reduce vibration, Oilite bearings and super finishing for shafts. Chrysler also developed a road wheel with a ridged rim, designed to keep a deflated tire from flying off the wheel. This safety wheel was eventually adopted by the auto industry worldwide.

The advanced engineering and testing that went into Chrysler Corporation cars helped push the company to the second-place position in U.S. sales by 1936, a position it would hold for more than a decade.

The American automobile industry led the world for many decades before other countries' forays. Most notably, Volkswagen and Toyota gained significant market share during the '60s and '70s by focusing on cost and quality that didn't exist to the same degree in the United States. Although the U.S. remained a major player the game had been permanently changed – and they were struggling to keep up.

INSPIRED BY CRISIS

In 2008, the "Great Recession" hit. Things got so bad that in the middle of 2009 two major U.S. automobile manufacturers, including Chrysler (which became Fiat Chrysler Automobiles, or FCA, in December, 2014), declared bankruptcy. To survive, the leadership at FCA knew they had to make a dramatic change with their products, delivering much greater levels of precision manufacturing, quality control and collaboration.

Alan Whitted, from FCA, who we introduced in Chapter 4, illustrated this shift in focus to quality, precision and collaboration. "After we went through bankruptcy there was a big change in our approach and attitude toward quality. Before bankruptcy the stamping and die functions for parts at Chrysler acted as two silos. There was a lot of antagonism between the two groups and performance suffered. Back then we would be happy with parts out of tolerance that at times could be larger than 1.0mm (1 millimeter is about the thickness of a credit card), which was completely unacceptable. Post-bankruptcy we knew we had to work differently if we were going to produce better results, so the leadership started getting the two groups together, creating a collaborative mentality and approach. The result was the ability to consistently produce parts within the specifications of .25 and .50 of a millimeter." (.25 would be like slicing your credit card into 4 credit cards.) "That's a huge shift. There was a realization that in order to achieve the results we wanted, we needed to change how we worked together and how we respected our quality objectives."

Mark Battle, who we introduced in Chapter 3, had this to say about the shift in focus at the stamping and die group at FCA, "One of the critical functions of our work involves changing out dies" (customized tools that make specific parts). "The time it takes to make that change is very important. It needs to be done with precision and efficiency. Before the company went bankrupt, Automatic Die Change Time or ADCT, averaged 35 minutes per change, which was dismal by industry standards. Now, after three and a half years of working together with both the engineering and manufacturing groups to reduce that number, the average is 21 minutes. This means we're able to make 34 percent more parts in the same time frame. The faster you're able to make these parts, the more productive you can be and the more cost effective you are." Mark and Alan focused their teams on building collaboration and improving specific results in both precision and timing, two critical aspects of their work.

At Loews, Stephen Cummings reinforced the importance of creating and clarifying specific measurements when he told us, "We develop a business plan for all managers with specific goals that include team member satisfaction, customer satisfaction and profitability. There is extreme clarity, which helps us stay focused on what's most important."

MEASURING AND RECOGNIZING

When a team is focused on results, they are directing their energy and efforts toward accomplishing the agreements they've made. Measuring and recognizing these efforts serves as a way to observe progress as well as affirm and inspire continued effort. High performing teams want to know how they're doing. Is production where it needs to be? Are we meeting our quality standards? Is any part of our effort vulnerable right now? As we mentioned in Chapter 4, most people want to make a positive difference in the world. Measuring and recognizing achievements is the primary way to validate the difference the team is making.

There are a number of excellent resources in the marketplace that identify how teams should go about determining effective goals and creating the right metrics. Although it is important work our focus here is on the four benefits of measuring achievements and outcomes:

1. **It creates a sense of urgency.** When the focus of meetings and conversations are directed at who's doing what and what's being accomplished it builds attention and reduces complacency. This does not mean meetings and conversations should only be task focused, but like the yin-yang model from Chapter 1, high performing teams balance the Task and People dynamics by maintaining a healthy sense of urgency towards reaching their goals while maintaining trust and respect in the relationship.

2. **It helps the team avoid getting lost in the "trees".** High performers tend to be very focused on doing their individual part (i.e., the trees). While this is necessary on an individual level it can lead to forgetting the big-picture (i.e., the forest) and create silo thinking. Measuring and reviewing team perfor-

mance helps members stay focused on their collective achievements and reinforces the team's identity.

3. **It helps a team determine if they need to make adjustments**. When teams fail to measure their performance on an appropriate, regular basis, it is easy for them to miss critical junctures where they should course correct, alter timelines or adjust goals.

4. **It ties recognition to performance**. Teams that measure their achievements have the capacity to recognize individual and collective efforts in a way that links to performance. This enhances self-worth and reinforces desired performance.

Regarding recognition, there is a large body of research on the tremendous positive impact it has on performance. However, it's important to acknowledge a danger on this path. Measuring something while under the promise of big rewards or strong threats can easily lead a team to measure the wrong things. We worked with a call center leadership team several years ago that shared a story about a time when they tried to address a key complaint from customers: long wait times in the call center. They believed that by lowering wait times, they would be able to take more calls and provide more efficient service. So naturally, heavy attention was given to daily reports and substantial weekly rewards. Not surprisingly, they were very happy a few months later when call times had dropped by about 50 percent. Complaints about wait times were virtually non-existent.

However, complaints about levels of dissatisfaction increased dramatically. Customers were no longer waiting as long for service, but felt rushed on the call and felt their complaints were not being thoroughly addressed. So the leaders of the call center did more research and discovered three deeper issues:

1. Representatives had disparate perceptions of the appropriate way to process concerns.

2. Online resources of standardized answers were heavily underutilized.

3. Reps with less experience were relying on those with more experience for answers instead of finding the information themselves from the appropriate source.

Once the call center managers addressed these issues, wait-times remained low and customer service levels significantly improved. Measuring wait times wasn't a bad idea, but it was a misleading metric to focus on and recognize.

IMPACT OF BEHAVIOR PATTERNS

When it comes to focusing on results, it's important to keep behavior patterns in mind. Consider the difference between *what* is accomplished and *how* it is accomplished. For example, people with certain behavior pattern preferences enjoy getting the full details of a task clarified before taking action, while others prefer getting only enough information to get started. These different approaches can be complimentary on a team but they can also create tension that needs to be proactively managed for a team to experience ongoing success.*

Recognition is another area where it is important to be mindful of behavior patterns. Many recognition efforts mistakenly focus on the recognition preferences of only one or two patterns, which can lead to exactly the opposite effect from what's desired. For example, focusing mostly on the quality of the work is more meaningful for those with an analyzing preference, as opposed to those with an influencing preference. For an individual with an influencing preference, that type of recognition is less affirming and can actually be demotivating. On the other hand, giving those with an influencing preference a "high-five" and enthusiastically telling them how much you appreciate the great job they did (sincerely, of course) will most likely have a positive impact on them, but have a demotivating impact on someone with an analyzing preference.

LOOKING AHEAD

By measuring their outcomes and achievements, a team can determine the "why", "what" and "how" behind the measurements. This mentality also directs the team's attention to fixing problems (future focused, where do we want to go and moving forward) instead of fixing blame (present or past focused, where we are or have been and are stuck).

One of Bank of Hawaii's most senior and respected executives, Wayne Hamano, Vice Chairman and Chief Commercial Officer, told us how changes in the bank's management style included this change in focus. "It used to be you were judged on what you had done in the past for the bank. Now we're focused on what you are contributing today and how that helps the bank get where it wants to go rather than what you've done before. That way no one can rest on their laurels."

Andrew Tisch, from Loews, recalls something else he learned from Bob and Larry Tisch, who built Loews Corporation. "Learn from your mistakes but don't let them overwhelm your future judgment." This doesn't mean a team shouldn't be honest and acknowledge current problems and challenges, but focusing on what happened creates a myopic, past-centered perspective. Focusing on the past is about blaming and defending; focusing on the future is about problem solving to meet the clear and common purpose.

Therese Dickerson, Vice President and Human Resources Manager of the Talent Development department at Bank of Hawaii also spoke about the bank's shift towards performance (i.e., results) and the subsequent impact it made. "In 2000-2001, we made a critical shift in our focus. Before then, our growth strategy was purely focused on geographic expansion, but when we took an honest look at the locations where we had expanded, we saw poor performance. In analyzing the reasons it became clear that our growth strategy was pulling our attention away from our geographic and cultural strengths. We were expanding for the sake of expanding, which wasn't an effective strategy. We took a step back and made some big changes, closing our poor performing offices in California, Nevada, Australia, Asia and the Pacific Islands. It wasn't the most uplifting time in our history, but this change allowed us to eliminate inefficiencies which improved our overall performance and hone in on our most valued client base, Hawaii. Today, we focus on results, collaboration and quality, emphasizing execution much more now than in the past. Performance matters and it's recognized by the Forbes top ranking year after year."

DAVID VS. GOLIATH

An unusual and precedent-breaking decision was made in the world of nuclear physics in 2008 by the U.S. Department of Energy (DOE). The DOE announced that it would build the Facility for Rare Isotope Beams (FRIB) at the National Superconducting Cyclotron

Laboratory (NSCL) at Michigan State University (MSU) instead of at its own Argonne National Laboratory.

"Like David felling Goliath, a relatively small university lab beat out a much larger national lab in the competition to host a $550 million accelerator facility for nuclear physics," wrote Adrian Cho in the December 2008 issue of the Scientific Community Magazine.

(Before we go any further, a little context on rare isotopes might be helpful. Briefly stated, rare isotopes are short-lived atomic nuclei that are no longer found on Earth. Most of the current research in nuclear physics relates to the study of these nuclei under extreme conditions such as high spin and excitation energy. Researchers are able to create these nuclei with artificially induced fusion or nucleon transfer reactions by employing ion beams from accelerators that increase the energy of a beam of particles. Rare isotope research is expected to have a tremendous impact in our understanding of the origin of stars and planets and dramatically improve the diagnosis and treatment of some diseases, including cancer, along with the stewardship of nuclear weapons.)

When we spoke with Thomas Glasmacher, the Project Director for the Facility for Rare Isotope Beams at MSU, he gave us some background on the study of rare isotopes. "The U.S., Japan, Germany and France have been the global leaders in rare isotope research, but Japan was poised to surpass the U.S. in isotope research capability. The U.S. nuclear science community convinced the government that the nation needed an advanced rare isotope facility, and in 2008 the Department of Energy (DOE) announced a competition for $550 million to fund the building of a world-leading rare isotope facility. MSU was interested in hosting this facility, but accelerator facilities of this scale have always been located at national laboratories." In fact, since the early 70's national laboratories have been the exclusive province of high intensity accelerators and the primary recipients of federal government funding for nuclear research. One of those labs, Argonne National Laboratory, had already announced it would enter the DOE competition. A university like MSU was thought to have no chance of winning.

But that's precisely what happened when the DOE made its decision in 2008 and announced that MSU had been awarded the project instead of its contractor, Argonne National Laboratory. How did this happen?

Any time there is a major achievement involving many different parties there are a lot of variables involved, and this was certainly the case for MSU. Thomas elaborated on one of those variables when he explained, "Over the years, NSCL has reinvented itself three times. At first, it was a proton facility, then a heavy ion facility, and then a rare isotope facility in the 1990's. The lab has a group of faculty and staff who are committed to each other, committed to nuclear science and committed to being the best scientific user facility and center for education of the next generation of scientists, demonstrated by how they have been reinventing the laboratory". Having a team of people that were so focused on what the customer (i.e., the scientific users) needed that they were willing to change direction and had done so multiple times, was a critical variable in their success.

Another crucial factor was being part of a major university like MSU. Founded in 1855, MSU was used as the prototype for the Morrill Act of 1862 that donated public lands to several states and territories for colleges teaching agriculture and the mechanic arts. MSU was the first among those newly created institutions of higher learning in the United States to teach scientific agriculture.

More recently, U.S. News & World Report ranked MSU:

- 75th among the world's top 100 universities,

- 35th among the nation's public universities,

- 1st in the nation (for 21 straight years) for graduate programs in elementary and secondary education

- 1st in the nation for undergraduate program in supply chain, and

- 1st in the nation for graduate programs in nuclear physics (of which the NSCL is a key driver), organizational psychology, and rehabilitation counseling.

Being a part of a university with a long history of academic strength and having a president (Lou Anna K. Simon) that was fully invested were essential components of success. This investment wasn't just talk; President Simon and the MSU Board of Trustees made substantial financial commitments to support the project if they were selected by the DOE.

Given the highly technical competence required for work of this nature, it would be naïve to say that a focus on results was what won the DOE competition, but it certainly played a major role. The clear focus and actions of the proposal team along with the other various groups helped create one of the necessary paradigm shifts that allowed MSU to win the proposal instead of Argonne. As Thomas said, "There is no question that our team needed to deliver a compelling proposal. This required us to make sure all our actions were clearly focused on success. Different agendas could not be allowed."

* **Note:** *Effectiveness Institute offers a half-day workshop, Leveraging Team Dynamics, that focuses on ways a team can manage these differences to their benefit.*

KEY POINTS – FOCUS ON RESULTS

Teams exist to get something done, so it is important that they ***measure and recognize achievements and outcomes.*** There's an old adage that says, "that which gets measured gets done". This practical wisdom helps the team determine the "why", "what" and "how" of what needs to be measured. One caution: be sure you're measuring the correct things. Focusing on results also helps the team stay directed on problem solving with an eye on the future. This leads to achievement, accomplishment and completion.

When achievements are recognized self-worth is enhanced, commitment increases, focus remains sharp and energy remains high. A critical variable in successful recognition is being aware of the recognition preferences of the different behavior patterns in people.

QUESTIONS ABOUT RESULTS

How are team progress and accomplishments measured and communicated? Are the efforts of all team members measured equally?

_____

_____

_____

How are team members recognized for their accomplishments? How does recognition motivate you?

_____

_____

_____

What level of volatility exists in your working environment that impacts deadlines? What external variables impact deadlines? How do you plan for or manage these uncontrollable aspects?

_____

_____

_____

How is appropriate urgency for results established and communicated?

_____

_____

_____

Is the current level of performance sustainable? If not, what needs to change?

_____

_____

_____

_____

CHAPTER SEVEN

Alignment of Authority and Accountability

The sixth and final characteristic in the Teams That Work model includes a number of important variables for high-performance teams. These variables are packed into one characteristic because of the critical first word, "alignment". When there is alignment of authority and accountability, all team members are doing their part to reach the team's overall purpose.

A simple story about the impact of alignment came from Sharon Crofts, Vice President of Operations and Technology at Bank of Hawaii. "When I began managing facilities in 2010, we had just had an unacceptable report from internal audit. Instead of taking a confrontational approach with the audit team, which was common at the time, I asked team members to align their thinking and behavior with the audit group and engage with them not as a group that created problems but as teammates that helped us identify and correct problems. Making this shift was a challenge but our next audit was remarkably improved and the process was much smoother. Clarifying our alignment with the audit department's work created a collaborative effort that made a huge difference in the outcome."

We've been fortunate to observe and work with many excellent teams over the years, but for this characteristic we're going to center our attention on the remarkable work of a relatively small team at a very large company.

EAST MEETS WEST

Hard to believe, but in 1970 commercial air travel was virtually non-existent in one of the largest nations. Today China boasts the world's second largest number of commercial aviation passengers. Many factors have been involved in this dramatic change in such a relatively short time frame, but one factor was the assistance of The Boeing Company.

The roots of Boeing's relationship with China can be traced all the way back to 1916 when William Boeing hired China-born Wong Tsoo as the company's first chief engineer. The relationship was reenergized in 1972 when President Nixon visited the country and introduced Boeing aircraft to a nation that was beginning to emerge from decades of underdevelopment. Then in 1993, a milestone in this long term relationship was reached when an agreement was made for Boeing, in cooperation with Chinese airlines and the Civil Aviation Administration of China, to provide enhanced professional training to Chinese aviation professionals. Some of the areas of training included pilot skills, flight operations, maintenance engineering, air traffic management, executive management, airline management and marketing, manufacturing, aviation safety and quality assurance, finance and industrial engineering. To date, a rapidly growing number of over 50,000 professionals have received this training.

One team at Boeing that plays a key role in this initiative is the China Strategy and Integration Training Team (CTT), which develops and delivers learning events for executives from airlines, airports and regulatory agencies within the various regions of mainland China. The cross-cultural nature of this work, combined with a complexity of potential subjects and the variety of potential client interests create a substantial risk in "getting it right" for the groups that arrive in the

U.S. for these events. With all these variables, meeting client needs is rarely a straight forward process, so CTT must be flexible and nimble while maintaining high levels of professionalism. The stakes are also very high; their client is one of the largest and most influential nations in the world.

Maintaining trust and respect, while achieving high levels of ongoing success with so many dynamic variables, is challenging. CTT has had to be crystal clear on the alignment of authority and accountability between team members. However, this does not mean team responsibilities aren't shared. In fact, CTT has intentionally designed their team so more than one person has the skill set required to perform the various roles, such as instructional design, logistics coordination, production, course facilitation, program administration, and training program lead. Assigned roles change depending on which learning event the team is working on, but their structure allows for backups as well as preventing silo thinking. And this wasn't the first time Boeing employees assumed authority to augment a limited set of responsibilities with their own interpretation to provide greater meaning and effectiveness.

ROOTS OF THE PRECEDENT

Back in 1929, William Boeing's business was rapidly growing as the science of aviation was changing. Wood and fabric were giving way to metal frames and aluminum skin, and "streamlining" was the buzzword of airplane design. Major competitors, such as Ford and Fokker, were building bigger tri-motor transports. But Boeing Chief Engineer Charles "Monty" Monteith felt that a smaller, faster transport that took advantage of the latest technology might be the way to go.

That revolutionary airplane, known as the Monomail, made its first flight in 1930. The smaller plane was difficult to design and, like many new ideas, was not readily accepted. However, William had made it clear that he wanted his people to take risks. During an interview earlier that year, he said, "I've tried to make the men around me feel, as I do, that we are embarking as pioneers upon a new science and industry in which our problems are so new and unusual that it behooves no one to dismiss any novel idea. Our job is to experiment, to let no new improvement pass us by." The leader of Boeing had set a precedent. Define one's own responsibilities consistent with the overarching objective of the company or the team. The specifics are up to individuals to determine.

CTT members shared an example of how they align their work with high level strategies. When they were asked to design a senior executive training, they developed a curriculum with renowned speakers from around the country with expertise in global competitive strategy and cross-cultural business relationships. That curriculum was approved by a Boeing Executive Council. Meanwhile, the Boeing China office, in discussions with the customer, discovered the great importance Chinese government leaders place on using aviation as one of the key drivers of economic development. When the CTT heard this, they re-thought the entire curriculum. They worked closely with the Boeing China executive and subject matter experts as well as the Stanford Graduate School of Business to develop a program that tied economic development to aviation, innovation and global business success.

Having to re-think the entire curriculum and the stress that created could have easily eroded levels of trust and respect between team members, but that didn't happen. By being clear on their overall objective and how their individual actions impact the functions and activities of other team members, CTT has learned how to take action in ways that raise the probability of success in achieving their purpose.

NOT BECAUSE I SAID SO

Practically speaking, alignment of authority and accountability means all team members act on defined roles and expectations. For this to happen, three things need to be clear.

1. Authority Level

   When levels of authority are well understood, everyone has the authority they need to act on their defined role. This does not mean everyone needs to have autonomy in the decision making process, but it does mean they have the authority they need to fulfill the expectations of the role. In addition, they are clear about the authority level other team members have for their roles and expectations. This type of clarity reduces confusion that can slow team performance.

   One important point on authority; there is a difference between professional and personal authority. Professional authority is given to an individual based on position, area of expertise or responsibility. Personal authority is related to others' perception of values and how they are expressed in behavior. It is possible to assign professional authority, which is the focus of this section, but lack personal authority because of issues related to trust and respect.

   In our work with teams we've found the following scale to be helpful in identifying and clarifying levels of authority. (**Note:** Depending on an individual's knowledge and experience along with the skill level required for a task, an individual could start by having a level of authority anywhere on the scale.) The following example focuses on an imaginary decision-making, development process to illustrate one way the scale can be used to clarify levels of authority. One clarification: the numbers only serve as names of the five categories and are not intended to be hierarchical or value related.

1	2	3	4	5
Me	You influence me	We	I influence you	You

Imagine a complex task that you have deep knowledge and experience with. It is highly possible that you would function at category 1 on the scale with that responsibility. At this level you have full autonomy for making decisions about that task, and although you could seek input from others before making a decision you would not be expected or required to do so. This category is not always appropriate or possible (think of possible safety or regulatory requirements), but it is the most empowering and expedient.

Now let's say you are going to train someone to take over that task and this individual has no related knowledge or experience. Initially the person you are training would likely start at quadrant 1 where they have no authority because they do not have the knowledge, talents or skills to make decisions. In other words, you would continue to be the decision maker and would not consult them before making decisions.

However, after they begin the learning process the individual would hopefully move to category 2 in the decision making process. At this point you would continue to make the final decision but would not do so without getting input from the person you are training. This would begin building that person's confidence for making the decision on their own and help you discover what knowledge they may still need to acquire.

Category 3 authority reflects consensus decision making. Depending on the task, you may or may not move to this category with the person you are training, but if you decided to make decisions here you would both have equal decision making authority. In other words, decisions would not be made until you both agree on the decision, or are willing to support it. Because this category requires mutual agreement it can be very powerful, but it is also the most time intensive.

Once you are confident the individual has sufficient experience and knowledge to make good decisions you might move to category 4. Here the two of you would discuss decisions before they are made but they would have authority to make the final decision.

If the individual reaches the point where they can make decisions without your input they would be able to work at category 5. They might seek input of others but are not expected or required to do so before making the decision.

One note of caution for categories 1 and 5; it's never a good idea for team members to look unprepared or uninformed, so if you make a decision that could create that impact make sure they know ahead of time...especially the boss!

The point is not to diagnose every task of every team member on this scale. The purpose of the scale is to present one way to clarify levels of authority team members have for tasks. When authority is clearly aligned in a way that allows team members to act on defined roles and expectations there is typically an increase in a sense of empowerment and innovation.

Skip Sack, former Executive Vice President of Applebee's International, shared a colorful story about the impact his level of authority had on innovation. Skip developed Ground Round, the first casual dining chain in the country. "When we first started Ground Round we'd put a basket of popcorn on top of a basket of peanuts on the tables. Then we put popcorn machines in the dining rooms under a return air duct so the smell would waft through the restaurant. Naturally, the first thing a customer would do would be to reach for the popcorn because it didn't have to be shelled. Eating the popcorn was addictive so it took time for the guest to get to the peanuts. By the time they did, they were pretty much full. Our cost for peanuts and popcorn was half the cost of what we spent on peanuts alone."

Jan deRoos, Associate Professor and HVS Professor of Hotel Finance and Real Estate at the Cornell School of Hotel Administration, shared how his department has "an enormous amount of freedom to define what success means. This was not imposed on us by the institution. The faculty, working in cooperation with the industry, was able to define that success". Freedom aligned with clear authority creates empowerment and a pathway for increased innovation.

2. Clear Expectations

Everyone on the team is clear about expectations – not only their own but also those of other team members (to the degree that is necessary to eliminate confusion). When clear expectations are combined with commitment to a clear and common purpose, clarity around expectations eliminates the deadly "that's not my job" energy from the team. However, for expectations to be clear they need to be understood, specific, realistic and confirmed. Many times at least one of these four variables is missing, which can result in team members working hard to achieve a result that was not desired.

Also, team members need to be clear on the "why" behind the expectations. Understanding "why" provides context for "what," and on some teams, this important variable is the difference between success and failure. When "why" is unclear, the door opens for doubt, which is the beginning of behavior that erodes trust. Left unaddressed, this type of confusion and ambiguity creates a breakdown in team performance.

3. Ask for Accountability

    Even when team members work hard to make things clear, misunderstandings and mistakes can still happen. So the final aspect of the alignment of authority and accountability is to be clear on and agree to how team members will "ask for accountability" when appropriate. When a team member doesn't do what was expected or doesn't do it to the level agreed to, there is a need to ask questions that build understanding and problem solving. Otherwise it can appear the expectation didn't matter. However, if team members don't agree and incorporate how they are going to ask for accountability, trust, respect, commitment and results will suffer.

    Part of clarity on asking for accountability is agreeing on whom to go to when an accountability conversation is needed. Some teams defer all accountability conversations to the manager.

While this is an option and may be culturally required, in the Teams That Work model all team members go directly to each other when there is an unmet expectation. This allows the team to perform at higher levels.

You may have noticed that we said "ask for accountability" instead of the more commonly stated "hold someone accountable". The reason for this is that "holding" assumes a power position that does not build full ownership for tasks. It also reduces the dignity of the other person and typically impacts the level of trust and respect in a negative manner.

The power of clear alignment and the way it can benefit an organization is illustrated by this closing story from Wayne Hamano at Bank of Hawaii, who we introduced in Chapter 6. "Two years ago one of our branches, staffed with 23 people, produced $80 million in loans. This past year, at the same location, we produced $223 million in loans with only 12 people at that location. The change in volume required much greater clarity of alignment of authority and accountability, as well as an increase in delegation. Everyone has to be productive. When team members' authority, expectations and accountability are aligned to a commitment to a clear and common purpose, great things happen."

KEY POINTS – ALIGNMENT OF AUTHORITY AND ACCOUNTABILITY

Deferring to the boss to hold team members accountable is a natural, hierarchal tendency. But in Teams that Work, each team member *acts on defined roles and expectations* that align with the team's clear and common purpose. With this type of thinking and behavior everyone asks the questions that lead to accountability.

If team members are going to act on defined roles and expectations, they need four things:

1. They all "**have**" the authority they need to accomplish their part in achieving the purpose.

2. They all know "**what**" each other is accountable for. It is everyone's responsibility to ask questions that lead to accountability.

3. They all know "**why**" each other is accountable for what they do. Without accountability, the team breaks down, energy scatters and productivity is lost.

4. They all know and agree "**how**" to ask for accountability when something isn't done or done correctly. This is different than using position power to "hold" others accountable. Asking for accountability is simply asking questions about the defined roles and expectations that were clarified and agreed to while establishing the clear and common purpose.

QUESTIONS ABOUT ALIGNMENT

If team members do not have the authority they need what is preventing it from being given?

_____

_____

_____

How does authority (personal or professional) impact the ability of team members to "get the job done"?

_____

_____

_____

Do all team members know what everyone is accountable for and why? If not, what needs to be clarified?

_____

_____

_____

How does the team have accountability conversations? Is there agreement on guidelines for these conversations?

_____

_____

_____

What constitutes an equitable distribution of the workload between team members?

_____

_____

_____

CHAPTER EIGHT

Applying Teams That Work

As you've read this book you probably noticed the interdependent nature of the six characteristics. For example, it's counterproductive for team members to "act on roles and expectations" (alignment of authority and accountability) without a commitment to a clear and common purpose. That would be a bit like trying to drive a car in a straight line with tires that are severely out of alignment. So if a team is going to apply the characteristics to improve performance where should they start?

Before we answer that question it's important to recognize that the characteristics in the Teams That Work model are listed in the order of how people tend to talk about challenges in team performance. Team members rarely say "we aren't aligned" or "we don't have difficult conversations" or "we don't have a clear purpose." When there are problems on a team the most common statements center around issues related to trust and respect, which is why we began with those characteristics.

However, trying to improve team performance by starting with a focus on increasing trust and respect between team members is ineffective because trust is an outcome that's built as team members work together collaboratively day in and day out. Going away on a "trust-building" retreat can be helpful, but if the other characteristics aren't present, that trust will be paper thin when workplace pressure inevitably hits.

If a team is going to apply the model effectively they should focus on characteristic 3: commitment to a clear and common purpose. This characteristic is the cornerstone of the model. If there is misalignment here, all of the other characteristics will be negatively impacted.

Once a team has clarity and commitment of purpose they should focus on characteristic 6: alignment of authority and accountability. This characteristic provides clarity about how the team will go about fulfilling its clear purpose.

When 3 and 6 are clear the team should turn their attention to characteristic 4: willingness and ability to manage conflict (i.e., ask the difficult questions), and 5: focus on results (i.e., measure and recognize achievements and outcomes). These two characteristics are the ongoing actions the team performs once 3 and 6 are clear. Part of the clarity on these two characteristics should include making sure the team understands:

- What is going to be measured.
- How it is to be measured.
- Why it is being measured.
- How success and achievements will be recognized.

One final point on conflict – if team members do not have the ability to have constructive difficult conversations, it is critical to build these skills. When difficult conversations are not handled well, trust and respect will decrease.

Characteristics 1: high level of trust and 2: high level of respect are outcomes of the other four characteristics, meaning that once a team's purpose and roles are clear, they are focused on results and are asking the difficult questions effectively, trust and respect develops. As we mentioned in the trust and respect chapters, knowing the different behavior patterns of team members and how these impact individual relationships and team performance is critical. Respect can also be enhanced when team members increase their awareness of the technical competence of other members through cross-training.

THE IMPACT OF THE LEADER

In Chapter 1, we promised to address the variable of leadership of the team. Although we won't do an deep dive into the topic, we need to mention it because the research we've conducted and reviewed confirms that *the largest single variable in team performance is the leader.* This is not to say there aren't other important variables that impact team performance, but the way the team leader acts and what he or she says has such a tremendous impact on team performance that it is difficult to overstate its significance.

One illustration of this point came from work we did with a company that has its roots back in 1916. That year, Harold Spinner started a small business selling wooden boxes to apple growers in Washington State. A century later, his company still provides boxes (cardboard) to the current generation of apple growers, who account for 60 percent of all apples grown in the U.S. The company, H.R. Spinner, headquartered in Yakima, Washington, is the largest privately owned distributor of packaging materials in the Northwest.

For 95 of those years, the company grew at the same rate as its market, between 5 and 15 percent, depending on how the weather impacted the yield of the apple crop. Then, the fifth president to preside over

H.R. Spinner, Ed Jewett, came to a realization. The company that his predecessors had passed down to him could no longer be run like a simple monarchy with him as sovereign.

This approach to management had existed since the company's inception. Although the company formation was a partnership, and there were six partners, one of the partners had always been designated President with responsibility for all operational, legal and financial decisions. Because of this high level of responsibility, Ed found himself tied to the office, no longer able to visit some of the company's larger clients. Ed recognized that being President should not require him to do all the work himself. He had to change the way he was leading the company.

Among his partners were two young men who yearned to do more. With the other partners' agreement, Ed made one Vice President of Operations and the other, Vice President of Strategic Partnerships. This would allow him to focus on the overall direction of the company and spend time with key clients whom he had been neglecting.

As Ed pointed out, the company wasn't used to change. Initially, there was a lot of anxiety and concern about the new structure. Ed needed to demonstrate in both his words and behaviors that this new direction was the way to the future, and included a "one for all and all for one" approach.

Slowly but steadily over a period of months everyone saw him focus on strengthening the relationships, and of course sales, from key accounts, while also allowing his new "lieutenants" to make decisions that previously sat in a very long line waiting to get his attention. What happened? Between 2012 and 2014 sales grew 81 percent!

While every situation won't see these kinds of financial results based on leadership behaviors, the story illustrates the importance of a leader demonstrating in words and actions the behaviors they want to see. For a leader of a Team That Works this means consistently modeling behaviors that support the six characteristics.

APPLICATION FOR VIRTUAL AND PROJECT TEAMS

One of the questions we're often asked is how the characteristics change on a virtual (also known as distributed or remote) or project team. The simple answer is they don't, but there are variables in these two types of teams that impact the characteristics.

For example, the purpose and roles on a project team along with the lines of authority and accountability are often determined before the team is established, so the process of clarifying characteristics 3: commitment to a clear and common purpose and 6: alignment of authority and accountability are expedited. However, as you might recall from Chapter 4, having a clear and common purpose does not mean project team members will give their full discretionary performance for project success. That still requires commitment.

Also, some project teams may not be together long enough to build high levels of trust and respect. As long as the team is meeting their milestones and quality standards for deliverables a moderate level of trust and respect may be sufficient for a short-term (i.e., 1-2 months) project.

Research on distributed or virtual teams has revealed that the biggest challenge is building trust, so unique steps are often required to build characteristic 1: trust. Since visual information strongly influences trust, it's especially important to make sure team members have and use technology that allows them to see each other, which is one of the best practices of virtual teams.

CLOSING SUGGESTION

Effectiveness Institute offers two excellent tools to help teams apply this model to improve performance: the Teams That Work Toolkit and the Teams That Work Plus⁺ program.

1. The Teams That Work Toolkit and accompanying assessment focuses on the team's perception of the team. The Toolkit contains the following elements:

    •   Two 30-question online, Likert scale assessments based on the six characteristics that capture and synthesize how team members perceive the team's performance. (The first assessment is for initial discovery and the second is taken 3-6 months later to determine progress and results of the team's efforts to improve performance.)

    •   A Leader Guide that outlines a step-by-step process for the team to debrief their results and create an action plan. (The word "Leader" does not refer to the team leader but to the individual that will lead the team through the debrief process. It does not require certification or extensive preparation.)

    •   A Participant Workbook for each team member that facilitates their participation in the debriefing and action planning process.

    •   A PowerPoint deck with embedded video that guides a team through the debriefing process and explains the Teams That Work model.

2. Because of the critical impact a leader has on a team, we also offer the Teams That Work Plus⁺ program and accompanying assessment. This Teams That Work Plus⁺ assessment includes the team's perception of the team and the team leader's perceptions. This provides the team information that includes:

- The team's perception of the team.
- The team's perception of the leader.
- The leader's perception of the team.
- The leader's perception of the leader.

The Teams That Work Plus⁺ program contains:

- Two 36-question online, Likert scale assessments based on the six characteristics that capture and synthesize the various perceptions outlines above. (Like Teams That Work, the first assessment is for an initial discovery and the second is taken 3-6 months later to determine progress and results of the team's effort to improve performance.)

- A Participant Workbook for each team member that facilitates their participation in the debriefing and action planning process.

- A PowerPoint deck with embedded video that guides a team through the debriefing process and explains the Teams That Work model.

- One note: the Teams That Work Plus⁺ program requires delivery by a certified facilitator. Certification, which includes the Teams That Work Plus+ Facilitator Manual, is available through a train-the-trainer process.

For more information on either of these options please visit our website at www.effectivenessinstitute.com or contact us at 425-641-7620.

KEY POINTS AND QUESTIONS SUMMARY

CHAPTER 1–TEAMS THAT WORK
KEY POINTS

Teams That Work is based on a model of six characteristics of high-performing teams. The degrees to which the six characteristics are present indicate how well the team performs. At a macro level, strong team performance requires balancing both Task, or technical skills, and People, or relational skills. The Teams That Work model helps teams determine how to find and maintain an effective balance between the Task and People aspects of performance.

Among the variables that impact team performance, there are two critical ones addressed in this book: behavior patterns and the behavior of the leader. These two variables will be seen throughout the discussion of the six key characteristics:

1. High level of trust.
2. High level of respect.
3. Commitment to a clear and common purpose.
4. Willingness and ability to manage conflict.
5. Focus on results.
6. Alignment of authority and accountability.

QUESTIONS ABOUT TEAMS THAT WORK

1. Before learning more about the six characteristics, which one do you think your team is currently doing well? Why do you have that perception?

2. On which of the six characteristics do you think your team needs the most work? What experiences have created that perception?

3. How is your current team doing at balancing both Task and People skills? Does it focus on one more than the other? If so, what is the impact?

4. Based on the brief descriptions of the different behavior patterns, which quadrant, or quadrants, do you believe you prefer? Which quadrants do you think your fellow team members prefer? What are the implications for team performance?

CHAPTER 2–HIGH LEVEL OF TRUST
KEY POINTS

Trust ties into the chemistry part of the relationship. Trust means I am willing to be open to you. This does not mean I need or am expected to share things about my personal life, but it does mean I am willing to share my knowledge, talents, skills and experience with you for the benefit of the team and team members.

Three things must be present before I will be willing to be open to you:

1. A perceived integrity. You play by rules around courtesy, professionalism and respectful treatment. It is about doing the right thing for me, for the team and for the organization.

2. A perceived authenticity. What I see is what I get. You are experienced as real and genuine. There is a pattern to your behavior that allows for predictability so I am not surprised or hurt.

3. A belief that you care. I believe you care about me, the team and getting results.

QUESTIONS ABOUT TRUST

1. Trust is tied closely to values. Upon what values are the team's decisions and actions based? How is this demonstrated?

2. How do team members define integrity?

3. When a team member doesn't do what he/she says they will do what is the protocol for addressing it?

4. What actions demonstrate caring to you? What impact does that have on your willingness to be open?

5. How do you define honesty? What do you do when you believe someone is not being honest?

CHAPTER 3–HIGH LEVEL OF RESPECT
KEY POINTS

Respect ties into the talents, skills and abilities that an individual brings to the team. It is linked to the fact that you are good at doing something. I have a high regard for your ability to use your talent and skills.

Although trust and respect are related, they are not the same thing. Someone may be a trustworthy person, but not technically skilled for the job they have been hired to do. Or an individual may be technically brilliant but untrustworthy.

Also, trust and respect don't happen easily or automatically. Trust and respect are earned over time when you work together on a task. When both trust and respect are present, team members have what they need to truly rely on each other.

QUESTIONS ABOUT RESPECT

1. What talents and skills (technical, strategic, interpersonal, etc.) do you hold in high regard?

2. Are the talents and skills you identified in #1 the same that other people see when they work with you? What are the variables that impact this?

3. How does respect impact the level of engagement team members have with each other? What actions demonstrate engagement?

4. In what way does respect from others (or perceived lack of respect) impact your team's performance?

5. What types of opportunities exist for team members to provide input on team decisions, and how are these handled?

CHAPTER 4—COMMITMENT TO A CLEAR & COMMON PURPOSE KEY POINTS

When team members are fully invested in a goal that everyone understands, they are all in on the purpose.

- We use the word Clear to eliminate misunderstandings. Misunderstandings occur when everyone uses the same words, but the words don't mean the same thing. "Take care of it" does not mean the same thing to everyone. We have to be clear in our communication or team members can't be sure what the expectations are.

- We use the word Common to make sure everyone is on the same page. We need to agree on the priority, the resources and the urgency.

- We use the word Purpose because it is "higher order" than a goal. Achieving the purpose is fulfilling the larger intent, while completing a goal is simply accomplishing the task (e.g., the purpose is to attract and retain world class talent; the goal is to expand our selection process outside the region.)

It is one thing to make something Clear and quite another to have it be Common. Clarity by itself gets interest: "I will do it if it is convenient." All in is about commitment – there are no excuses, only results. Three elements are needed to reach this level:

1. Discussion about and connection to something that is larger than self.

2. There's something in it for me – personal integrity, belonging to something larger than me, achievement of the goal, making a difference.

3. There's room for disagreement. The discussion and resolution of disagreement begets the clarity that is the cornerstone of trust and respect.

A commitment to a clear and common purpose creates true collaboration while preventing splintering and silos from forming within the team.

QUESTIONS ABOUT PURPOSE

1. What is the team's purpose? How do you know the purpose is clear to all team members?

2. To what degree is the purpose of the team reflected in the behaviors and actions of the team?

3. How much are team members willing to personally risk for the purpose to become reality?

4. In what way do your values align (or not align) with the team's purpose?

5. How do your priorities align (or not align) with the team's purpose? How do the other team members' priorities align (or not align) with the purpose? What needs to happen to align everyone's priorities?

CHAPTER 5–WILLINGNESS & ABILITY TO MANAGE CONFLICT
KEY POINTS

Resolving conflict is a counter-intuitive behavior in our culture. Team members must be willing and able to ask the difficult questions and address the issues.

If conflict is not addressed, it simply goes underground where it lingers, grows and negatively impedes the development of trust and respect. The challenge is to surface, discuss and resolve conflict so that all energy goes into goal achievement.

There are two tendencies to resolving conflict that are not productive:

- Ignoring the conflict (flight).
- Becoming overly aggressive (fight).

Neither extreme works because they both fail to addresses the issues or feelings underlying the conflict. If the feelings are not addressed and resolved, they fester. These unresolved negative feelings will reappear, usually with greater intensity and with a destructive force. And if the issues are not addressed the team performance suffers.

QUESTIONS ABOUT CONFLICT

1. In what way does the team create (or not create) an environment of mutual effort and open communication for talking about frustrations or concerns?

2. Does the team tend to move toward difficult conversations when necessary, or avoid them? Why is that your perception?

3. If the environment does not seem safe enough for you to ask difficult questions, what needs to change?

4. How would you rate your skill level at managing conflict effectively? How would you rate your team member's skills?

5. Having productive difficult conversations requires focusing on a future desired state that fixes problems rather than a past-focused state that leads to defending, justifying and blaming. Where do your team's difficult conversations tend to focus?

CHAPTER 6–FOCUS ON RESULTS
KEY POINTS

Teams exist to get something done, so it is important that they measure and recognize achievements and outcomes. There's an old adage that says, "that which gets measured gets done". This practical wisdom helps the team determine the "why", "what" and "how" of what needs to be measured. One caution: be sure you're measuring the correct things. Focusing on results also helps the team stay directed on problem solving with an eye on the future. This leads to achievement, accomplishment and completion.

When achievements are recognized self-worth is enhanced, commitment increases, focus remains sharp and energy remains high. A critical variable in successful recognition is being aware of the recognition preferences of the different behavior patterns in people.

QUESTIONS ABOUT RESULTS

1. How are team progress and accomplishments measured and communicated? Are the efforts of all team members measured equally?

2. How are team members recognized for their accomplishments? How does recognition motivate you?

3. What level of volatility exists in your working environment that impacts deadlines? What external variables impact deadlines? How do you plan for or manage these uncontrollable aspects?

4. How is appropriate urgency for results established and communicated?

5. Is the current level of performance sustainable? If not, what needs to change?

CHAPTER 7–ALIGNMENT OF AUTHORITY & ACCOUNTABILITY KEY POINTS

Deferring to the boss to hold team members accountable is a natural, hierarchal tendency. But in Teams that Work, each team member acts on defined roles and expectations that align with the team's clear and common purpose. With this type of thinking and behavior everyone asks the questions that lead to accountability.

If team members are going to act on defined roles and expectations, they need four things:

1. They all "have" the authority they need to accomplish their part in achieving the purpose.

2. They all know "what" each other is accountable for. It is everyone's responsibility to ask questions that lead to accountability.

3. They all know "why" each other is accountable for what they do. Without accountability, the team breaks down, energy scatters and productivity is lost.

4. They all know and agree "how" to ask for accountability when something isn't done or done correctly. This is different than using position power to "hold" others accountable. Asking for accountability is simply asking questions about the defined roles and expectations that were clarified and agreed to while establishing the clear and common purpose.

QUESTIONS ABOUT ALIGNMENT

1. If team members do not have the authority they need what is preventing it from being given?

2. How does authority (personal or professional) impact the ability of team members to "get the job done"?

3. Do all team members know what everyone is accountable for and why? If not, what needs to be clarified?

4. How does the team have accountability conversations? Is there agreement on guidelines for these conversations?

5. What constitutes an equitable distribution of the workload?

About the Authors

Tom Champoux, Co-Founder and President of Effectiveness Institute, is a nationally recognized and dynamic speaker, energizing trainer and executive coach. The heart of his work lies in creating an organizational culture built around empowerment and the exchange of trust, respect and dignity. Tom addresses national conventions and annual meetings on such topics as "The Changing Role of Leadership," "Teams That Work," "The Power of Trust, Respect & Dignity" and "Navigating Conflict."

Cliff Chirls, Managing Partner of the Effectiveness Institute, is also an executive coach focusing on operational excellence. Through strategic insights into the people strengths, market position and material resources that organizations possess he helps clients build great businesses. He has 30 years of technology industry management experience, has published articles on various information processing topics, and has written on the collaboration of marketing and sales in firms where those two functions' interests typically collide. He is also the inventor of our patented phone app.

George Myers, Senior Partner and Consultant, is an expert facilitator and presenter with over 25 years of team, leadership and organizational development experience. With a professional background in retail, higher education, technology, finance and service industries along with his direct work with various leaders at all levels in those organizations, George has gained a broad understanding of the challenges facing leaders and teams. This knowledge informs his work overseeing the development of the Effectiveness Institute's programs.

Wake Technical Community College
Health Sciences Library
2901 Holston Lane
Raleigh, NC 27610-2092

DATE DUE

GAYLORD · PRINTED IN U.S.A.

CPSIA information can be obtained
at www.ICGtesting.com
Printed in the USA
LVOW10s1851161117

556557LV00012B/1133/P